STORIES FROM THE EDGE

"Thank God for Dave Wiles, a bruised human being wh~ ~~~~ ~ds, through troubles in his own life and through his ~~~~~~~~ ~ed lives of others, that Christianity is a m~~~~~~~~~
         – Adrian anc

"*Stories from the Edge* shows us where C~~~~~~~~~ ~~~ ... This is invaluable for those who are enga~~~~~~~~~ ~. work."
    - Nick Shepherd, Executive Team Leac ~~~ ior Youth Ministry

"A good story enthrals, inspires and challenges. *Stories from the Edge* does all of these things."
    - Nigel Pimlott, Author of *Youthwork After Christendom*

"Dave's passionate, long-term commitment to the youth of our nation pulses through this book."
    - Matt Wilson, National Director, Eden Network

"Dave not only practises what he talks about, his own story shows the impact that can be made. A moving, challenging and motivating read."
    - Tim Evans, CEO, Worth Unlimited

"Be warned – this book doesn't hold back; it is not a gentle read! Instead, it is full of tough stories and the reality of the lives of young people on the edge. The brilliance of the book is in the questions – challenging the assumptions we have when working with young people and encouraging us to be people of grace and hope."
    - Jill Rowe, Oasis Ethos Development and Resourcing Director

"Direct, real, and personal."
    - Richard Passmore, Author of *Meet Them Where They Are At*

"Will inspire, challenge, disturb and encourage you."
    - Louise Kenyon, Nazarene Theological College, Manchester

"An amazing collection of stories ... A refreshingly honest and down to earth read for anyone who shares Jesus' heart for people on the margins."
    - Gavin Calver, National Director, Youth for Christ

"Powerful and very important."

– Rt Revd Roger Sainsbury, former Bishop of Barking

"A compelling account of what it means to reach out to young people on the margins. There are no easy solutions and no quick fixes but through it you get a compelling sense of what it means to "do justice and love mercy".

- Ian Sparks, OBE

"Fascinating and challenging. Dave writes eloquently from his own experience and offers insights that show both God's transforming power and ways of doing youth work with integrity."

- Dr Sally Nash, Director, Midlands Centre for Youth Ministry

"Stories get under our skin like nothing else can. They leapfrog our prejudices, swish past our fears and poke our souls with a truth we cannot ignore. Dave Wiles' brilliant collection of stories will spark animated conversations and deep reflection."

- Jenny Baker, co-founder of the Sophia Network

"Dave Wiles himself is a great story. He is also a teller of great stories - of honest, persevering Christians offering the hope and comfort of redemption and renewal to troubled young people."

- Dr Bob and Annette Holman

"Everyone loves a good story and this book is packed with them - stories that challenge, inspire, shock and pull the rug from under your feet. It had me gripped."

- Jonny Baker, Mission Leadership and Communities Team, Church Mission Society

"Dave Wiles demonstrates his passion for telling the story of people's lives and how they connect with the big story of a God at work in all our lives."

- Paul Fenton, M.A., Dip.H.E., Oasis College Principal

"The stories have a very broad appeal. I'd recommend it to any Christian who loves people. It's a book with dark bits, but leaves you feeling hopeful and positive."

– Jon Birch, www. asbojesus.wordpress.com

STORIES FROM THE EDGE

Dave Wiles

MONARCH
BOOKS

Oxford, UK & Grand Rapids, Michigan, USA

For Donna, Daniel, Hannah, Joe
and, of course, Harry

First published in the UK in 2010 by Monarch Books
(a publishing imprint of Lion Hudson plc)
Wilkinson House, Jordan Hill Road, Oxford, OX2 8DR, England
Tel: +44 (0)1865 302750 Fax: +44 (0)1865 302757
Email: monarch@lionhudson.com
www.lionhudson.com

ISBN 978 1 85424 963 0

Distributed by:
UK: Marston Book Services, PO Box 269, Abingdon, Oxon, OX14 4YN

The text paper used in this book has been made from wood independently certified as having come from sustainable forests.

British Library Cataloguing Data
A catalogue record for this book is available from the British Library.

Printed and bound in the UK by MPG Books Ltd

Contents

Frontier Youth Trust

Frontier Youth Trust (FYT) is dedicated to mission with young people at risk, helping them to work towards justice, equality and community. Based upon direct experience of youth work and research FYT also supports, resources, informs, advises and trains those working with and on behalf of disadvantaged young people. As a Christian network dedicated to advancing the Kingdom of God, FYT believes that the most effective youth work is built upon Christian principles.

For further information about FYT's work please see: www.fyt.org.uk

Thanks

I would like to offer sincere thanks to my whole family, particularly my brothers and sisters, for their love, support, understanding and tolerance!

Thanks also to the authors of the short "Stories from the Edge" that are included in this book. They are: Paul Hobbs, Debs North, Bernie Comissiong, Pete Hope, Dave Horton, Isla Horton, Matt Robinson, Chris Bristow, Bev Palmer, Matt and Diane Hall, John Walker, Jo Fitzsimmons, Nigel Pimlott, Paul Hazelden, David Swain and Stephen.

Special thanks to my FYT colleagues and Directors, who remain an inspiration and encouragement. Particular thanks to Tim Evans (Worth Unlimited) who helped me write Chapter 5. Thanks also to Pat Offer and Howard and Paula Thompson for the use of their homes to get the space to complete this book.

Finally, thanks to the youth work legends who are central to the narrative and development of my own story: Jane Sellars, Jim Davis and Audrey Browne, along with Bob and Annette Holman, who have always had such a significant role in my life.

A Word of Caution

Some of the material in this book is of a sensitive nature and it may raise issues for you in relation to your own past, or other concerns that you may have. Please do talk to a trusted friend or seek other appropriate support and help if this is the case.

Foreword

by Adrian and Bridget Plass

George Reindorp, Bishop, master storyteller and broadcaster was fond of talking to us about the politeness of Christ. He pointed out, for instance, the occasions on which Jesus would begin his stories with the words, "What think ye...?" This, he explained, was an invitation to his listeners to sort out the meaning of a narrative or parable for themselves. Being bashed over the head with teaching, however accurate or worthy, has never done anyone much good, in our experience. Story, because it is quite happy to exist and justify itself purely on the level of entertainment, allows a privacy of response that can be deeper, more considered and often more challenging than preaching in its most negative sense. This book does not offer a set of definitive answers to questions about interaction with troubled young people. Rather, it creates opportunities for reflection and discussion without the debilitating, lowering presence of those twin ogres, correctness and resolution.

Thank God for that. And thank God for Dave Wiles, a bruised human being who understands, through troubles in his own life and through his involvement in the battered lives of others, that Christianity is a messy business. Like all the most effective followers of Jesus that we know, Dave walks a very narrow path himself, but his arms are open wide to receive the puzzles, the disappointments, the pain and the continual, if infrequent, delights of seeing how the practical love of God can bring real change in hopeless situations. The mess has to be embraced.

In this connection we should mention that we have a couple of things in common with Dave, quite apart from the fact that we all think Christians should be doing as well as talking. Adrian and Dave have both had to reconcile negative images of male parenting with the picture of God's fatherly love as presented by Jesus in the story of the prodigal son. Dave's description of the journey he has made towards forgiveness of his now deceased father is one of the most moving accounts we have read for a very long time. God never did drop a neatly packaged solution into his arms, any more than he has yet sorted things out for Adrian in that area. It is a work in progress, and a pattern for the majority of work done with people in trouble. No easy answers.

Which brings us to the other thing we have in common. All three of us have worked with teenagers in residential care. Some kids, particularly the ones in secure units who had been labelled violent or likely to abscond, laboured under unimaginably complex burdens of confusion and neglect. In the parable of the sower Jesus said that some seed fell on stony ground and was unable to grow. The process of breaking up stone and creating good soil in the hearts of those children was never going to happen without long-term commitment and a readiness to work through the one-step-forwards-two-steps-back syndrome that Dave describes at one point in these pages. Both of us, like Dave, have had the corners knocked off our approach to ministry by real contact with real people, and we thank God for that.

Dave's aim is to affirm, encourage, inspire and challenge those who work with folk in need. *Stories from the Edge* will certainly do that. We commend this book to you.

Introduction

This is a book of stories. Anthony De Mello, exploring the power of stories, writes: "it is a great mystery that though the human heart longs for truth, in which alone it finds liberation and delight, the first reaction to truth is often hostility and fear."[1] He points out that spiritual leaders like Jesus often employed stories to circumvent the opposition of their listeners. It may be common to oppose truth, *but it is impossible to resist a story*. Those leaders knew the power of language. "Once upon a time..." are such entrancing words!

Story, then, is the main medium of this book. The stories are interspersed with reflective theological and theoretical questions and comments that seek to explore aspects of the narratives. Academics would call this "praxis". The book is written in a way that is intended to bring you into the story; to enable exploration of your experiences, thinking, values and world-view. The book seeks to enable you to sharpen, refine and develop your own capacity to relate with love and understanding to those around you.

This book is written for those who are interested in people, who perhaps work alongside others (in any capacity). It may be of particular interest to those working with children, to youth workers and to community workers of all types. It is written to affirm, encourage, inspire and perhaps challenge in terms of how we serve and are served by the human race – those we are commanded to love. However, I hope that it will also have a wider appeal and interest to anyone who just likes a good yarn!

The stories come from a number of sources: some are based on my own story of growing up; others are reflections from my experience as a youth and community worker. There are also stories from other youth workers, and some of the stories have been taken from the broader tradition of story-telling. Where possible I have acknowledged the source of each story. Several, however, have come from anonymous sources, and if the author of any of these contacts me, I will be happy to acknowledge them in future publications.

In a couple of sections I have drawn on material that I have covered in other publications. This is due to the relevance that the material has for the themes covered in this book.

Each chapter is thematic and is written in a similar structure. Chapters begin with a short reflective story followed by some of my own personal story; this is followed by questions, theory and other stories for broader discussion. The chapters then go on to tell the stories of other youth and community workers, with discussion questions based on their experiences.

So, if you're sitting comfortably, we'll begin...

Chapter 1

Offending Behaviour, Dads and Lads

Once some robbers came into the monastery and said to one of the elders: "We have come to take away everything that is in your cell." And he said: "My sons, take all you want." So they took everything they could find in his cell and started off. But they left behind a little bag that was hidden in the cell. The elder picked it up and followed after them, crying out: "My sons, take this, you forgot it!" Amazed at the patience of the elder, they brought everything back into his cell and did penance saying: "This one really is a man of God."

Thomas Merton, *The Wisdom of the Desert*[2]

The start of my story

"I believe that he did it as a type of symbolic action. He was paying society back for taking his father away and putting him in prison."

This was how the probation officer was explaining my behaviour to my mother. This was the way in which he wanted to report my delinquency to the courts when my case came up the following week. I thought that it sounded good – a dead certainty in hooking the sympathy vote from the magistrates!

In later years, I reflected that the explanation did indeed hold water, even though it was probably less than half the story. I was indeed resentful about my Dad not being around. I was tired of "jailbird" jokes from my friends. I was fed up with being singled out to receive free school dinners – in front of the whole class! And why did I have to go to those awful Christmas parties that the local philanthropists felt obliged to inflict on us, the deserving poor? Why was I paying the price for my father's crimes? Why was it that my brothers and sisters had to suffer because of his misdemeanours? And most importantly to me, why was my Mum having to put up with it all on her own?

The trouble had started a week before. It was a cold Sunday morning and a friend and I were kicking around our neighbourhood. There were too few of us to merit a game of football and it was too cold to hang around the streets with no entertainment. We decided to investigate the newly built bungalow up the road. Hanging around building sites had always been a favourite pastime: long before adventure playgrounds, they provided the stimulus that we craved: walking the high-wire scaffolding, playing chase amongst the half-finished walls of someone's living-room, or avoiding the inevitable attention of the local policeman who had been called out to investigate the noise!

The bungalow was in pristine condition, ready to receive its first proud owners. If it was money we were after, our undeveloped criminal minds had let us down – the bungalow was unoccupied! We broke in anyhow, discovered our mistake and decided to try our hands at decoration instead of burglary. Back in the 1960s, there were no "makeover" TV programmes to inspire our efforts, so we resorted to contemporary psychedelic, using the paint that the decorators had left behind.

It was at this point that a knock at the door interrupted our activity. As mere fledgling villains, we made the mistake of answering it! The policeman was not as impressed with our artistic efforts as we were. So, several weeks later, the probation officer arrived to write a social inquiry report about me.

The report never did get the sympathy vote that I had hoped for. For this, my first offence (well, the first I'd been caught for!), I was given a two-year probation order. Perhaps the magistrate knew who my father was. All the police officers I had ever had dealings with certainly did. "You're Bob's boy, aren't you?" was the standard question when our paths crossed.

Perhaps the magistrate was trying to rescue me by sentencing me to see a probation officer. However, it confused me. I thought it was punishment, but it never felt like it. Anyway, whatever was intended, the two years of probation only made me resolve never to get caught again. I was nearly successful.

An evolving life of crime

One near miss came with my Dad when I was sixteen years old. I had started my second job since leaving school and was now a builder's labourer. I knew where the cement was kept and my Dad, a builder himself, wanted to use my "insider knowledge" so that he could get some cement for free. So late one night we went to the cement shed. I opened it with the key that was always left under the same stone, and we began to load up Dad's car with bags of cement.

This was nothing new to me; I quite enjoyed the occasional "job" with my Dad. Other kids enjoyed trips to football matches or the cinema with their parent; for me, it was safe-breaking or relieving some shop of stocks that he presumed were surplus to requirements.

So there we were, by the light of the moon, surrounded by houses, quietly loading the bags into the boot of my Dad's car. It was a smooth, almost military operation; our silence would have made the SAS proud. However, this was about to change!

As I dropped the last bag into the car, my Dad slammed the boot shut on my fingers! I realized the importance of silence and hissed at several decibels that he should open the boot, pronto! However, it had locked and the keys were in the ignition, awaiting a swift getaway. Hence, it was several long minutes before I was released and we were able to make our way to the hospital to fabricate some story about my fingers getting trapped by the car door.

Father and son, and thoughts of God

My relationship with my Dad had not been easy. Maybe I resented him coming home from prison and usurping the sense of responsibility that I felt for my four younger brothers and sisters; or maybe I was jealous of his relationship with my mother. Perhaps he was jealous of my role in the family. For whatever reason, I didn't think that he liked me and he certainly seemed to demonstrate hostility towards me whenever I stepped out of line.

Having trained in social work later on in my life, I realized that I could easily have ended up in care or on an "at risk" register if anyone had disclosed the degree of violence that he dished out to me. Of course, he was the product of Victorian attitudes about parenting, which meant few physical demonstrations of affection, a "stiff upper lip" mindset, and a belief that children should be "seen and not heard". I grew up wondering if I meant anything to him at all. Many of my contemporaries felt the same way about their parents.

He tried to drum religious commitment into me by ensuring that, along with my brothers and sisters, I prayed every night, and he sent me to the local Sunday school. However, this religious behaviour didn't seem to reconcile with my experience of him. Perhaps the impressions of fatherhood that I was getting from him were influencing my concept of God. Looking back at my view of God at that time, there was something badly wrong. My overriding perspective was that God was like my Dad and was only interested in discipline, control and punishment. I wonder how many other people are left with a distorted image of a "Father God" based on the fallibility of human parenting.

One afternoon I remember losing consciousness after my Dad had punched me from one side of the kitchen to the other. I vaguely remember coming round and seeing the trail of blood that marked my passage across the kitchen floor and thinking how bad I must be to deserve such treatment.

Tragically, this is the case for many children and young people who are abused (whether physically, emotionally or sexually): they believe that they deserve what happens to them. They assume that they are the transgressors, that they must be bad, wrong or evil. This untold damage lasts long after the blows have ended, or the night-time visits have subsided – on into adolescence and adulthood. The echoes of abuse can be detected in cyclical violence or an overbearing sense of guilt and insecurity which can manifest in a range of damaging behaviours.

> *I wonder how many other people are left with a distorted image of a "Father God" based on the fallibility of human parenting.*

On other occasions he slapped my face until I could feel no pain. However, bitter vitriol burnt deeply in my emotions and was waiting for its own opportunity for expression in some area of my own, or someone else's, life. My mother would often cry at these times, torn between her concern and love for me and her loyalty to the man to whom she had stayed so faithful throughout the years they had been together. It was a fidelity that endured, despite the twenty-plus years that he was away from us and in prison.

It wasn't until after my Dad had died that I came to a sense of restoration in my relationship with him. My family and I were devastated to hear that Dad had just a few months to live when he was diagnosed with lung cancer. On the surface, he had no fear of death; this was mainly due to his many years as a practising spiritualist. He was not too enamoured at the prospect of the dying process, but was not afraid of death itself. As children we had engaged in séances, holding the upturned glass as it rushed around the letters spread around the table, spelling out messages from those beyond the grave.

On occasions he would talk with a spirit who claimed to be his first wife, Julie. Whilst we children held the glass, he would ask questions of her that only he and she would know the answers to. The glass would flash around the table, spelling the names of places and people from their shared past – a past that we children could never have been aware of, as it happened years before we were born. He had his evidence for the afterlife and so death held little fear for him. His beliefs were home grown – a hybrid of spiritualism and Christianity.

When I became a Christian, his main concern was that I had accepted a distorted Christian belief about the person of Christ. My Dad understood him to be a son of God, like everyone else on earth – a great prophet, but not the incarnation of God. For many hours we chewed over this debate. I argued for a traditional view of Christ, one in which he is the only begotten Son of God (paradoxically, truly human and yet truly God), the Second Person of the Trinity, and the Redeemer of humankind.

Arguments abated when I heard of my Dad's terminal illness, and we concentrated on what we had in common. I wished him a place in heaven, and we would discuss what it might be like – "Gold in its rightful place, as a pavement, instead of ruling the hearts and minds of men!" He even agreed to build a dry-stone wall around my small plot in heaven, ready for when I arrived!

So it was during one of our conversations that he asked if he could be baptized. I was both thrilled and intrigued. When we talked about why he had decided to take this step, I discovered that it was because he had started praying to Jesus in person. He said that he was talking to him, man to man. In my supposed theological superiority, I decided to test his conversion

status by asking him what Jesus said to him when
they spoke. He replied, "He doesn't say much. He just
listens!" The answer struck me as profound. It was a
real joy to know that he had begun to experience the
Jesus who meant so much to me.

> *"He doesn't say much. He just listens!"*

He was baptized a few weeks before he died.
During that time I thought long and hard about whether I should talk to him
about the hurt that I still felt, based on his past treatment of me. However,
it seemed more important for me to dwell on the many good memories that
existed alongside the painful ones, rather than open old wounds.

On the day of my Dad's death, the family gathered around his bed. His
breathing was terribly laboured as the lung cancer reached its advanced
stages. We felt a common bond of helplessness in the face of his pain.
Holding my Dad's hand and forming a circle of hands with my brothers,
sisters and mother, I simply prayed that God would take him.

My eldest brother handed me Dad's King James Bible and asked me to
read. I didn't know what to read. Psalm 23 came to mind, but it seemed too
trite. I resorted to opening the Bible and reading whatever my eyes alighted
on. I could barely believe my eyes and ears as I read this:

> *Let not your heart be troubled: ye believe in God, believe also in me.
> In my Father's house are many mansions: if it were not so, I would
> have told you. I go to prepare a place for you. And if I go and prepare
> a place for you, I will come again, and receive you unto myself; that
> where I am, there ye may be also.*
>
> John 14:1–3 (KJV)

It was at the moment that I read "I will come again and receive you unto
myself" that Dad sat bolt upright in his bed, looked to the bedroom window
and died. I confess that it felt stage managed, as if God had opened the
curtains and called out, "Come on, Bob – it's time to go."

Father and son – redemption

My family reacted in differing ways to this special occurrence. Whilst grief was our collective experience, there was also a sense that we had witnessed something important, something that we would treasure as time passed. It caused us to wonder at the many and varied ways in which God works. Not for the first time, I would wonder at the sovereignty of God's response to prayer. I am grateful for his mercy and help, yet remain aware that this is not everyone's experience.

And so several years later, I sat in a hotel room, working away from my own home and growing family, and for some reason thinking about my Dad. I was pondering the many aspects of my attitudes and experiences that had been distorted by the harm that he had subjected me to. I was experiencing a cocktail of confusion, bitterness, hatred and fear. How much of what he had done and meant to me would be visited on my own children? Would I harm them by becoming what I had grown to hate, or would I be so scared of disciplining them that they would know no boundaries in their own lives? I decided that the only way I could respond would be to externalize these concerns and talk to my Dad as if he were in the room with me.

I set an empty chair across the room from myself and began what I assumed would be a monologue of my own self-pity. I spoke gently to my Dad, expressing all the things that I couldn't say to him as he died. I asked him, why had he made me feel so bad? Why did he not see that I needed his love and affection as much as his discipline? Why had he hurt me so much, both physically and emotionally? I cried as I alternated between calm words of condemnation and shouts of rage at his treatment of me and my mother, brothers and sisters.

However, the strange thing that happened was that my monologue became a kind of dialogue; it was as if he were actually there with me in the room. I sensed his own sorrow at what he had done to us as a family. Without any sense that he was abdicating responsibility, I seemed to hear the many reasons which helped to explain his behaviour. I "heard" his own sense of rejection and fear, his own feelings of inadequacy, the times he had been betrayed, harmed, rejected and hurt.

It began to make some sense to me; we had been part of a loop in history, a cycle of unbroken damage visited across generations as parents and children played out the scripts that they had inherited from the harm done in the past. The sins of a previous generation were visiting the next generation.

Fragments of stories that he had told me about his own past came back to me. His adoption; the cruelty of his relatives; the time he ran away from home at twelve, without even a pair of shoes; his travels; the crimes that he had been involved in. They weren't stories that I wanted to hear. However, as I accepted some understanding about his past and his posthumous apology to me, I experienced a calmness and peace that had been alien to me moments before. A degree of restoration seemed in place.

Forgiveness is a process, not an event

I think one the most profound insights that I have gained about the nature of forgiveness has come from black friends in South Africa, in the post-apartheid years. Pastor Tommy Solomon once told me that forgiveness was a process as well as an event. A wise philosophy, which the South African people have adopted as they have brought past injustice to light in their Truth and Reconciliation hearings. It has to be said that this has been my experience, as I reflect upon my relationship with my father. I hope that Dad has found the grace to forgive me for my many shortcomings too. Forgiveness is a process that continues as I uncover emotional hooks that are left in my life. For example, perhaps the need to obsessively please other people is a substitute for not feeling that I ever pleased my father. These invisible barbs often tug at our inner life unrecognized, to our detriment.

Some further thinking, reflections and stories

This book charts my involvement in crime, violence, drug use, drug dealing and a range of other antisocial behaviours associated with many of the youth cultures that I grew up around in the 1960s and 70s. I guess a key question is, why did I do it? Here are some of the *possible* reasons that I have identified as I have reflected on my own past:

- ☹ My environment. I grew up on a council estate which had no community facilities. The only green space in the area was used to build garages. I was bored.

- ☹ My family was poor. I had three brothers and three sisters, and my father was not always at home with us.

- ☹ I was looking for prestige from my peer group, as I wasn't getting what I wanted in my family.

- ☹ I didn't get much recognition from school, despite passing my Eleven Plus. I didn't see school as my culture, or all that important.

- ☹ I was genetically predetermined to delinquency.

- ☹ My relationship with my father damaged me psychologically, or I was acting out the symbolic actions of someone who resented the loss of his father to prison.

- ☹ I was labelled by the police and courts because of my father's misdemeanours. This is what sociologists would call a systemic explanation of criminal behaviour and punishment. The system provided me with a label ("delinquent") and I lived up to it.

☹ The excitement of some of the television programmes that I watched inspired bad behaviour.

☹ My friends influenced me and led me astray. I would argue that they influenced me profoundly and that I colluded with their views of me in order to achieve the prestige that I desired. Sociologists and psychologists would call this peer pressure, or peer influence.

☹ It was just good fun and provided relief from the boredom that I was experiencing.

☹ Drug and alcohol dependency started to get a hold of me and affected my world-view and choices.

☹ I was influenced by the youth cultures that I associated with.

☹ I was (and am) a sinner! I made my own bad choices and walked in them.

☹ The church was irrelevant to me and was only interested in my spirituality rather than me as a whole person – for example, my needs for recreation or for my family to receive a fair income.

☹ I learnt how to behave badly from my father and my friends.

Of course, the list of why I offended could go on. Indeed, if we added to the list the other reasons for offending behaviour that we might be aware of, the list would be extremely long. My own experience has led to a number of personal insights that I believe are important in considering offending behaviours:

☺ Offending, as many sociologists would say, is multi-factorial. The danger is that we each carry around pet theories about why offences are committed by individuals. These are often based on anecdote, simplistic dogma, media speculation and personal bias. It seems to me that there are two extreme positions in terms of understanding offending behaviour. On the one hand, there are those who hold that the individual is solely responsible for their own actions and must be held personally accountable for all that they do. On the other hand, there are those who see the individual as held hostage to environment and circumstance – a kind of puppet, dancing to the tune of the environment. I would advocate that the truth, for any individual who has offended, lies in a different place on a continuum between personal responsibility and environmental factors and considerations. Thus, I would argue that individuals need responses to their offending which are based on a sophisticated understanding of them as an individual in their individual circumstances. I'd suggest that a broad and open understanding of behaviour is required and that the responses to offending behaviour need to take account of context, if we want justice for young people.

☺ Those who offend are also offended against. The "sinner" is also the "sinned against". For me this raises profound questions about the important themes of justice and mercy, punishment and rehabilitation, and responsibility and accountability. The judge, summing up on the crimes of two young girls who had savagely killed an older neighbour, sentenced them to many years of imprisonment, saying that they were "the products of an evil society" – that society was, of course, only subjected to the judge's verbal warning. Society and many of the institutions and systems that we have established to respond to offending (or the effects of offending) at times seem far from neutral. Black young people are over-represented statistically in prisons; more crime is committed in poor areas; young people who are "looked after" by a local authority do far worse than other young people in terms of educational achievement and employment.

☺ If you are interested in working with young people who offend, you need to know something of their story, something about their past. You will need to explore young people's own understanding of their experience. Attachment and rejection are two of the most foundational factors in human experience. They have a profound effect upon the way in which individuals experience, make sense of and live their lives. At times, of course, a psychotherapist, or other professionals, may be needed for individuals to explore and integrate their past experiences. Enabling a young person to reflect upon their past experience can greatly help them to understand their current life experience. But you may need to be in a relationship with them that is deeper than merely writing a report about them! How do we establish this kind of relationship?

☺ That the range of reasons for offending behaviour can be categorized as either internal (psychological and emotional) or external (environmental and sociological). To respond to one in isolation from the other is running the risk of putting out the fire upstairs whilst it burns away merrily downstairs. Young people may at times need an opportunity to unpack their feelings and behaviours through a psychodynamic approach. However, they may also need to be involved in planning how their neighbourhood is developed, so that it meets their needs as well as the needs of the Chamber of Commerce, the adult councillors and those who drive cars!

The challenge we face as Christians, in responding to offending behaviours, is to move beyond simplistic explanations and responses. We need to work for systemic justice as well as encouraging personal responsibility. We must respond to the whole person – body, mind and spirit.

A few questions for your own reflection

- What are your own views about offending? Do you think that there are any key reasons? Do you have a hierarchy of reasons? What has shaped and formed these opinions?

- What is the relationship between your own views about the reasons for offending and what you think should be done to those who offend?

- What theology, traditions and aspects of your own spirituality inform your understanding about offending behaviour and responses to it?

- How do you hear about and understand the background experience of the young people that you come into contact with?

Story from the Edge 1:

Paul Hobbs

The scene is a remand wing at a Young Offenders Institution in the north of England. When I came on to the main wing office, I found a keen young landing officer and an experienced probation officer in debate about an inmate. They both stopped in their tracks to ask me, as a prison chaplain, to go and see a lad of sixteen who they were sure was going to attempt suicide.

I did not waste time and within a minute I was walking along the landing to check out the situation. I reached the cell door and opened the flap, to see the young man with his head in his hands. I entered and lightly asked, "What's wrong?"

This guy did not really want to talk, but I employed my befriending skills and got him to talk a bit about himself and his situation. He had just come into prison again, not yet sentenced; he had been on heroin, his family had given up on him, nobody cared for him. He had a history of self-harm and he wanted to die.

I then gave him all the one-liners I knew: the value of life; small sentence, big life; you're worth more than this; surely someone must care; is there anything you want? But this kid was not buying what I was selling.

I told him that I cared, that I do this job because I care. He said, "You get paid for it." And, of course, he was right. I suggested that a worker deserves his pay. But he was not interested in me.

The conversation went on, and he explained that he had taken four days to decide that he was going to take his own life. And that was that.

I told him that I care because God cares, and God inspires me to care. He responded, "That's your opinion. I don't believe in God. I have my rights and I want you to leave my cell. I want to die."

At this, I might have left, but somehow I could not. I told him that I didn't want him to die, that I was bothered about him and just could not leave like that. We stayed in silence for a while. I was silently praying for the right thing to do. I was convinced he was going to try to kill himself.

"I don't believe in God. I believe in the devil and want to go to hell," he said. This stirred me to pray out loud: "Lord God, I pray for Jimmy and I ask you to show him your goodness. Please help him and let him know your love."

I found myself backing towards the cell door. I was longing for a change in behaviour, but he still wanted to die. I looked outside. The principal officer in charge of the wing was along the landing. I called him over and explained the situation. He gave his all to try and help. At the end of it he told the young man that he was not going to die on his wing.

We left twenty minutes later, having told the staff to watch Jimmy like a hawk, every few minutes. A little later the officers caught Jimmy trying to hang himself. He was relocated to the hospital.

The most important point is that for now, young Jimmy is still alive. But for how long? He still wants to die. He believes he has a right to die. His first sixteen years have taught him that. He is on the edge of life, and the life-support system, called the prison service, is doing its best. But it is inevitable that many will succeed in acting out their desires to finish the job.

Trying to save people like Jimmy, this far over the edge, is defying gravity. The saving actions and words must come much earlier in their lives, to give them and us a better chance. The weight of the years brings the decision. Trying to alter this is too often too hard. For me, seeing young men die, or trying to die, fuels my motivation to do something about it, to try to give some hope back, by some miracle of grace.

A few questions for your own reflection

- How do we deal with the stark reality of some people's despair?

- How do you decide when to try to give answers or when to stay silently alongside someone?

- Who do you turn to for help?

- How do you prevent some young people ending up with stories like this?

- Where do you get your support when you are worn down by the dejection and gloom that seem to overwhelm some of the young people we work with?

Story from the Edge 2:

Debs North

I have been working with Gary for a year or so now. I meet him in school socially, take him out of lessons to work on behaviour and do stuff outside of school with him. He's a nice bloke.

Darren is also nice and I've also been working with him for a year or so, doing the same kind of work.

Simon, Matthew, Rich, Steve, and Carl are in the same boat as Gary and Darren. The other things they all have in common are being in permanent trouble with authority, excessive drug/alcohol use/dependency and varying degrees of depression.

The problem is not in befriending these young men; it is not in tolerating their behaviour or being present whilst it happens. Neither is it in talking to them about what is going on, how they feel, or even where God might fit in. The problem is, I don't have much to offer them that they aren't already very cynical and jaded about.

Maybe I've been naïve up to now. Maybe, though I think I'm an experienced old dear, this is the first time I've encountered average working-class young men. Maybe the young men I have worked with before were exceptional and I shouldn't have based any generalizations on them. Maybe it's always been this way. Maybe... whatever.

> I just think that I'm seeing what it's like to be the third generation of post-sexual revolution, post-feminist, post-blah (add your own!) young men.

But I don't think so. I just think that I'm seeing what it's like to be the third generation of post-sexual revolution, post-feminist, post-blah (add your own!) young men.

Their grandfathers (my father's generation) were the first to feel the rough end of the wedge. Women started to look around and realize there were more possibilities than motherhood and a part-time job at Tesco's. Women started to leave unsatisfactory marriages. A "job for life" became a thing of the past and unemployment was rife. The goalposts of what it meant to be a man had moved. And men were left wondering, "What next?"

The young people's fathers (nearer to my generation) were still hopeful that with a nip and a tuck they might just manage. They got a trade or a profession with the knowledge that they would retrain when older. They worked hard at being nice to women and respecting us as equal(ish), and hoped that women would, in return, still marry them and have their babies. What they hadn't banked on was that those women would want careers, fantastic relationships and a comfortable lifestyle, and that the media would encourage them to have it all and to get it themselves. A man stopped being a necessity.

So that brings me to my boys. The men in their lives have often gone, or are busy working, or are depressed and clueless. As role models, they have shown their sons how to run away, be non-communicative or suppress all feelings. The real decisions in their lives are often taken by women – mothers, girlfriends, aunts and their mothers' friends. Women seem to be the ones calling the shots in their lives. The boys are very aware that the girls who are their peers are way ahead of them academically, emotionally, and socially. They are also aware that these girls, as bosses or girlfriends, will be in charge in the future. Traditional roles have gone and nothing has come in their place.

The future looks unknowable and this is why I would say that many of them are depressed. Two of my boys have been diagnosed as such, but the others also suffer from overwhelming lack of motivation, escapism, excessive anger, and a sense of helplessness. An example of all this, which amazes me, is that when they truant, it is not to go out with their mates but to stay indoors, curtains drawn, without drugs or confectionery, doing nothing. When they do go out, it's to get "off their faces". When I ask if it's fun, they say it's the only thing that stops them thinking about school, home and life.

So what am I doing about it? Well, I spend a lot of time just loving them to bits. I spend time listening and talking. I do fun stuff with them. And they do love it and respond really well. But at end of the day, I'm just another woman. I don't teach them how to be men.
Men who can see and plan for a future with and alongside women.

> So what am I doing about it? Well, I spend a lot of time just loving them to bits.

What my boys really need are blokes! Good, Christian, manly blokes to be their mates, to be their role models. Men who are prepared to get alongside them, drop piety and show them that men can be hard and soft, butch and gentle, tough and kind, a laugh and able to cry as well. I'd like to challenge you to be those things for the young men you work with. I think it's what Jesus might have done.

As a footnote, I do have to say that I don't think all of this is the fault of women seeking equal rights! The fault lies in men and women not being able to work it out together and women having to do it alone. The men have been left behind and need to start working out how to catch up.

A few questions for your own reflection

- What do you think? Is there a generational backlash relating to gender?

- What role do we have as youth workers in relation to gender issues?

- What kind of issues do we need to consider in relation to our own practice?

- What is happening to boys and young men where you work?

Story from the Edge 3:
Dave Wiles

What seemed to hurt him most was that no one seemed to understand. Why did they pick on him so much, just because his Dad was in prison? It wasn't his fault, was it? Didn't they realize how much they meant to him – his "friends"! Their rejection and hostility was twisting his young life into a bitter spiral of insecurity. Later in his life he would engage in attention-seeking behaviour that would lead to crime, probation, drugs and a string of meaningless relationships. Young people can be brilliant with each other, can't they? They can show real acceptance and openness with each other, but at times they can make some individuals really suffer.

I'm reminded of this youngster's story as I hear and see the drama in Bradford and other cities that are experiencing so-called "racial tension". It seems highly likely that many of these events are stage managed by individuals who have a vested interest in stirring up hatred between groups. But beneath the surface there is that powerful urge to belong. We all seem so dominated by an instinctive predisposition to tribalism. Of course, it all relates to the development of identity, the social construction of our perspectives on reality. Young people find meaning in gangs, in tribes, as part of the crowd, in fanatical support of football and other sports – but then Christians have their congregations, denominations, assemblies, conventions and so on!

> *But beneath the surface there is that powerful urge to belong. We all seem so dominated by an instinctive predisposition to tribalism.*

Many of the young men I have worked with have racist attitudes and some of them have acted out their violent reactions to people who are different from them. Where does it come from? Why do we fear those who are different? These are deep questions that we need to ask ourselves as we seek to help others understand themselves and those around them.

My own family background was strewn with ill-informed racist attitudes. My father was an active National Front supporter and in my early years I accepted those views as my own. The paradigm shift came for me when I experienced a profound conversion to Christianity and a sense of liberation and acceptance from a God who I knew was head-over-heels in love with everyone – no matter what their skin colour, gender, sexual preference or dress code!

That conversion led me into contact and dialogue with many people who are different from me. Imagine working alongside black young people, in a black township, during the years when apartheid was beginning to crumble. Deep changes in me began, and continue, as I try to understand where those irrational fears of difference come from.

It seems to me that an important function of youth work is to construct activities, arenas and processes where we can help people from differing backgrounds, cultures and experiences to connect with each other – to connect in ways that will help them to understand each other, tolerate each other and – who knows? – eventually perhaps learn to respect and care for each other. Some of the most profound learning experiences that I have had have been when working with groups of people who are sitting down to listen to each other – New Age Travellers and church people, young and old, people of differing faiths and those with none at all, drug users and prohibitionists, black and white.

A few questions for your own reflection

- What is the role of a youth worker in creating the kind of dialogue that I am suggesting?

- What skills do you need?

- Where do you start?

- If we accept some responsibility to be peace makers, how do we do it in our youth work settings?

- Do we understand our own prejudices enough to be able to use that insight to help others understand their own prejudices?

Story from the Edge 4:
Bernie Comissiong

What about parents?

"I've left home," Simon informed me. He was now standing on my doorstep with assorted bags filled with his earthly belongings. It was 8.30 on a Saturday morning, and the last thing I had expected on my day off was a visit from a seventeen-year-old who hardly spoke to me at youth club. I attempted to look unfazed as I invited him and all his "baggage" into my home.

Simon was a humorous and likeable lad. He was one of "the gang" but limited his subversive activities to fairly harmless pranks. Apart from his tendency to be a bit disruptive during youth group and overly energetic during social activities, there was nothing to dislike about him. However, to his father, Simon was out of control. His dad had phoned me on several occasions in the past to discuss Simon's behaviour at home. He claimed that Simon was unruly and rude and constantly broke house rules. I had only ever met Simon's father once and I had never been to his house, so I had never observed this behaviour.

Prior conversations with Simon's father had included chances to off-load frustrations, requests for help in maintaining disciplinary action (e.g. not allowing Simon to attend trips) and demands for me to give Simon a "talking to". However, Simon had always maintained that he didn't think there was a need for me to get involved. Until now I had trodden a fine line between a lad who hardly gave me the time of day in youth group and a

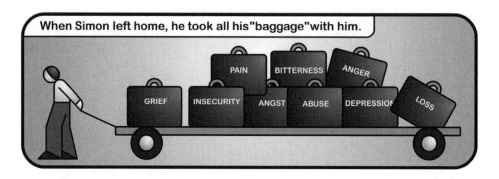

When Simon left home, he took all his "baggage" with him.

parent whom I hardly knew. My policy had been one of reacting to each incident as it arose and to offer mediation if they both agreed. However, Simon's father felt that my role would be to back him up as he told Simon how he should behave.

Now I had a teenager with all his belongings sitting in my living-room, eating my bacon butty and enjoying the novelty of listening to vinyl! We chatted about everything and occasionally we attempted to sort out a way through this present impasse. Finally, after lunch, his girlfriend arrived and they walked back to his parents' place. His home life carried on much the same for the next six months until he left the area. We laughed about the incident sometimes but I never did mediate between Simon and his dad. His dad phoned me on two other occasions to "talk", but that was as far as it went.

A few questions for your own reflection

- Can you maintain a relationship with a young person if you are acting as a mediator in a family matter?

- Can you help prevent incidents arising in a young person's family and also maintain a strong relationship with the parents?

- When is it appropriate to get involved in the family affairs of a young person you are working with?

- What guidelines should you introduce to ensure that you are not taking sides?

Story from the Edge 5:

Peter Hope

Kevin was described to me by his prison worker as a lovable rogue. He was a bit older than the lads we normally take on in Out4Good, but the thinking was, if he could turn it round he would make a good lead tenant for another house we had plans for in the future.

He was referred to me by a prison contact and I visited him twice in prison. He told me he had read Tony Anthony's book *Taming the Tiger*. He recounted how it had profoundly affected him, how he had prayed and "felt something", how he wanted to change, how he now saw how futile his drug-addicted life and persistent offending was, and how the dealers were out to rob his soul. He wanted to go to church when he got out of prison and learn about Christianity. His prison worker had said she had seen a notable change in him.

Kevin was also involved as a volunteer in the Keep Team in North Essex, an innovative police initiative that works with the voluntary sector to support and manage persistent prolific offenders in the community. It is an example of thinking outside the box, and the support worker the police have provided for Kevin has been a real asset to both Out4Good and the Keep Team. We have a burgeoning Christian community around the Out4Good house, a grouping of similarly minded people wanting to work with, support and love the forsaken.

On Kev's release, we welcomed him with a BBQ; normally he would have come straight out and scored on heroin within twenty minutes, thus going straight back into crime. This was a very different welcoming party. It was also the first time Kev had been offered supported accommodation; his life was panning out to be very different from the one he knew before he went to prison. He sensed a belonging and acceptance, and said so.

> there are always buts; the road to rehabilitation is a rocky, fragile one.

Working with the Keep Team, we had an initial full week's programme set aside for Kev, and activities planned for his first weekend. Everything appeared to be going great.

But, there are always buts; the road to rehabilitation is a rocky, fragile one. On the first Saturday after his release he received his community care grant. Temptation struck and he quietly left the house and spent most of the money on a massive drug bender over that weekend. He finally re-emerged late on the following Monday, remorseful and expecting to be asked to leave.

It was a confusing time for us all. We had decided through the experience of working with other lads that it was vital to get them into the house straight from prison and fill their days with activities. So it was with Kev. With his agreement, we provided as close a support programme as we could.

It is widely believed that the first three weeks after release are crucial when working with offenders who have had a drug habit before going to prison. We worked fully with all the other agencies, and we all shared the load and spent a lot of time with Kev. We had a comprehensive support plan written up and agreed. He was engaging with everyone; he was also enjoying being involved in the life of a committed church community.

At some point there was always the prospect of relapse, perhaps when the support started to tail off. But we didn't expect it so quickly, given the amount of initial support around him. It shook us all. I began to understand something more about the strength of the hold that drugs can have.

We accepted him back, gave him a written warning (as he had broken two of the house rules), and reiterated that living in the house was about committing to changing, giving up the chaotic life-cycle of drugs, crime and prison. Kev was adamant that he wanted to change, and he heeded the warning. Life settled down at the house, with Kev co-operating in all aspects of the support around him. He even proved to be a positive influence to the other young lads in the house.

> *He even proved to be a positive influence to the other young lads in the house.*

Kev's proudest achievements were in taking over the garden, which needed clearing. He dug a vegetable patch. He had no experience of gardening or tending a vegetable patch, but he took it on responsibly and enthusiastically. But one night his flourishing garden hit the radar of the local slug-and-snail community. The following morning, on his routine early inspection, he found his vegetable patch showing the highly visible signs of their presence. He was confused – he didn't know about slugs and snails or their capacity to wreak havoc and destroy young plants. When he planted the vegetable patch, he said it would be interesting to watch the plants grow in line with his growing faith – quite profound thinking, coming from a persistent prolific offender. Now he had something quite different to contend with – something unseen attacking the plants. This gardening malarkey wasn't going to be as easy as he had first believed. There was an obvious parallel between the attacks on his seedlings and his relapse and attempts to leave behind the chaotic world of drug abuse.

Kev continues to live in the Out4Good house. He is an ace cook – one positive skill that he learned inside! And he is working really hard at trying to stay off drugs. He is undertaking voluntary work, going to the gym, and getting involved with the local church and the wider Christian community. But he realizes that there is always something lurking, wishing to destroy the goodness that is growing in him and which is visible for all to see.

A few questions for your own reflection

- How many second chances can/should you give?

- How are we engaged in nurturing faith in folk like Kev?

- What metaphors might hold spiritual meaning for the young people you work with?

Story from the Edge 6:

Dave Horton

Recently I went to visit one of the lads I work with in a Young Offenders Institute. I was a bit apprehensive about the trip. I was looking forward to seeing him but also aware that he wasn't the easiest of young people to be with. He used to come to our weekly group sessions where we'd explore the meaning of life and the words of Jesus. He was quite often the most disruptive and the most hostile to the message we were hoping to share. Although he was capable of being friendly and respectful when "caught" on his own, when he was with his peer group (that is, most of the time) he was hard work!

Due to a friendly relationship with the chaplaincy team, I was allowed to sit in his cell for an hour and chat without the distraction of other family visits going on (and the watchful eyes of the "screws"!) in the visitors' room. We chatted about how he was getting on inside. We discussed how he might get on better *outside* after his release. Who might it be a good idea to avoid? What alternatives are there to the buzz of drugs and house burglary?

He told me about the lad in the cell next door to him. He had been sexually abused by a family member and had been left extremely damaged. He had already tried to commit suicide in the Young Offenders Institute. Because he had a low sense of self-worth, he never washed, and this meant that the other lads bullied him. My friend explained to me that he had decided to stick up for him, and had done this one day when his neighbour walked into the exercise room to the sound of taunts from other inmates.

I was amazed by this story. Could this be the same lad who'd sent me home weekly with a headache and a "Why do I do this?" question niggling in my thoughts? He seemed now to be living out some kind of real-life version of the Good Samaritan story! I told him that he was being like Jesus to the other lad. In fact I told him that in some way he was *being Jesus*

> *I was amazed by this story. Could this be the same lad who'd sent me home weekly with a headache and a "Why do I do this?" question niggling in my thoughts? He seemed now to be living out some kind of real-life version of the Good Samaritan story!*

to the lad. When I asked him if he'd like me to pray with him, he jumped at the chance. I thanked God for his opportunity to help his friend, I asked that he would have strength to do this, and I prayed about the changes he hoped to embrace on his release.

Two weeks after his release from the institute, I was walking through the local shopping centre with the same lad and some of his friends. As we passed the grocer's, he and his friends grabbed a handful of toffee-apples each and legged it. I was left standing outside, asking what has become a familiar question: "What am I supposed to do in this situation?" It seemed that my friend was struggling to live up to the promises and hopes he'd made for himself whilst inside. This "two steps forward, one step backwards" experience is common in youth work. At the end of the day, I have to trust that this experience was significant – a seed planted. A step towards Jesus. A sign of the kingdom of God?

A few questions for your own reflection

- Where and when might you be able to affirm the actions of young people and say, with all honesty, "Well done! That's what Jesus is like"? How often do you do it?

- Being open to Jesus in one environment won't necessarily translate to openness or interest in other situations. How do we help young people develop a faith that travels with them?

- How do you make sense of your youth work vocation when you so rarely get to see things sorted, tied up and solved?

Chapter 2

Fights, Flights and Drugs

The children were lined up in the cafeteria of a Catholic elementary school for lunch. At the head of the table was a large pile of apples. The nun made a note, and posted on the apple tray: "Take only ONE. God is watching." Moving further along the lunch line, at the other end of the table was a large pile of chocolate chip cookies. A child had written a note: "Take all you want. God is watching the apples"!

Source unknown

Earning a reputation

Two against one didn't seem fair odds to me, so, ever the people's champion, I dived in on the two guys who were attacking the lad at the bus stop. I don't actually think that chivalry had much, if anything, to do with my intervention – it was more likely the chance of a scrap! The first kid was easily scared as I head-butted him – his face showed his shock at my lack of Marquis of Queensbury tactics, whilst the blood gushed from his split nose. The other guy had to be chased down, and as I knocked him over to apply my Doc Martens to his head, the adrenaline left me no room to ponder the fact that he was about to spend the next four days unconscious in the local hospital. The bloodstains on my Prince of Wales chequered crombie coat were annoying, but at least they earned me a street name amongst my friends that met with my approval. I was named "Alex", in honour of the lead character in Stanley Kubrick's film *A Clockwork Orange*. A violent role model, but one that I did indeed look up to as a hero at the time.

Having explained in the first chapter that I am hoping that my Dad has been able to forgive me, I need to hold up my own hand in terms of some of my own misdemeanours. Of course, the reasons for my behaviour are complex, partially due to "nurture" (environmental factors), but they are also about my "nature" (personality and genetic make-up). In terms of trying to understand behaviour, perspective, the way that we see things, is crucial.

Good times too

As well as the painful times with my Dad, there were times that I thought of as fun – even though they were risky! His legacy to me wasn't just one of violence and anger. Sometimes there was a funny side to his illegal activities. On one occasion, we robbed a local business of its safe, but all we got for the backache was an empty safe that decorated his bedroom for years. It proved an interesting topic of conversation on the fairly frequent occasions when the police searched our house for stolen goods!

I have discovered the need for caution in recounting stories of my criminal past in front of my own children, as Donna, my wife, discovered to her embarrassment during a visit to our doctor one day. My son Daniel must have been about four at the time, and he had heard my testimony during a church service the day before. Daniel and Donna were waiting amongst the other patients in the waiting-room, in the kind of silence that only a doctor's waiting-room can inspire. It was a hot, sunny day, and Daniel climbed up on a chair to look through the window. With one foot on the window-ledge, he shouted across the room to Donna, "Is this how Dad climbed through windows when he was a burglar?" Donna did her best to ignore him and hoped that the others hadn't heard what he had said, but he proved most insistent with his question and only the bribe of some sweets rescued Donna from terminal embarrassment.

I often used to stand up for my Dad. For example, on one occasion I came to his defence in a fight with a neighbour. My Dad was in trouble, having gone to argue over my sister's reputation. I could see that he was losing. Being five foot nothing, he should never have tried his hand at fighting. I pulled the man away from my Dad, hoping that the fight would end. However, it was far from over, as he turned on me with a knife. My Mum spotted the knife and shouted a warning. Thankfully, several years of karate training took over my instincts, and I kicked the knife from his hand and broke his jaw without much conscious thought.

The mistake that I made was turning my back on him to walk away with my family. In the next few moments I literally saw stars as he pounced on my back, dragged me to the ground and began beating my face against the curbstone. A tooth came through my lip, and it was my turn to know the humiliation of defeat.

Not that this was to be my first or last defeat. On one occasion a couple of guys took it into their heads to threaten me for supposedly dancing on their car – they wanted money for damages for something I hadn't done. As I approached one of them for what I thought would be a friendly chat, I found myself left with a broken nose as well as a critically damaged ego, as I lay flat on the floor of the local disco. Later that week they met me in the gents' toilet of my local pub, and whilst two of them held me, the other laced into me – it felt very gang-land! My only comfort was that they never got a penny from me.

Hippy era

Then there were the drugs. "Far out, man – look at the grass!" I was with several friends, searching the damp grass at Stonehenge for something that one of us had dropped an hour or so before (we had forgotten what it was). To my eyes, which had somewhat dilated pupils because of the LSD I had taken earlier that evening, the grass had become a field of repeating patterns – fractal images in which diamond waves rolled gently back and forth to the sounds of the band. It was the 1960s and there was still a free festival at Stonehenge. This was in the days before relations between the hippies and the police had sunk to the low that they would eventually reach. So, when a police car's loud hailer made a good-natured announcement that "The sun will not be rising this morning, due to a lack of interest", a lot of us found nothing strange about the information.

The weekend before, I had been in Hyde Park listening to the Velvet Underground, whilst using cocaine. Hitch-hiking a lift back to my hometown of Bath, we arrived in time to play frisbee as the sun rose over the Georgian buildings of the city. It was a breath-taking experience – heightened, I'm sure, by the chemicals I had used – as I watched the hallucination of thousands of frisbees gliding across the city!

The following weekend I was in a state of dark paranoia, having used

LSD and opium too frequently. The evening had started off with a promising feeling; we had taken some tiny LSD tablets and walked to a friend's house for an all-night party. He lived in the countryside and so when I saw the glow-worms in the lane leading to his house, I experienced a lucid moment of clarity in which I imagined myself in a Tolkien-esque Middle-Earth landscape, accompanying hobbits and dwarves on some great adventure to the Lonely Mountains.

The experience turned sour in the early hours of the morning as I began to feel paranoid about smoking, imagining that my chilled exhaled breath was cigarette smoke, perpetually drifting in and out of my lungs. As I breathed I could see hot ashes and sulphurous fumes being emitted not only from my mouth but from the mouths of all my friends at the party. The only redeeming aspect of this experience was that it did eventually encourage me to give up smoking!

Getting involved in drug use

My encounter with drugs began at about thirteen years of age when I discovered that the drunken kick from cider worked more effectively when combined with certain pain-killers. By the time I was fifteen I had graduated to cannabis use, with good intentions not to use "harder" drugs. But my good intentions provided excellent paving-stones on the road to hell. I first tried cannabis in a roomful of friends who were experimenting with drug use together. I found the sense of euphoria and the lowering of inhibition, without the accompanying side-effects that alcohol provided, quite liberating. The

camaraderie of shared illicit activity was a bond of friendship that lasted many years, a bond which alerted me to the social and psychological dimensions of drug-taking, as well as all the other associated risks.

I even dabbled in selling drugs. However, this didn't last long, as I was too greedy. I laced the cannabis I was selling with herbal tea and charged extortionate prices, which made me very unpopular, to the extent that one man chased me around Bath threatening to knife me.

I even tried it on with the medical profession in an attempt to get prescribed drugs like Valium that we would occasionally use with drink to heighten the effect. I remember telling my doctor that I felt tired and lethargic all the time. I was sure that he would give me a stimulant of some kind and was overjoyed when I took the prescription to the chemist. A friend and I shared out the little red pills between us and took them all with an unhealthy dose of cider. After several days I discovered that the only effect of the tablets was constipation – apparently a natural side-effect from over-use of iron tablets!

Spirituality and drugs

For me, the use of mind-altering drugs was a way to explore myself and the world around me in a new mode of being. Whilst I believe there are as many differing reasons for drug use as there are for any other form of socially unacceptable behaviour, the exploration of my emergent self, and how I related to my friends and environment, were high on my list. Drug use became a kind of "spiritual burglary", or pre-emptive access to parts of my self that I believe are off limits in early life for good reasons.

As a Christian I believe that there is a "ghost in the machine". The complex array of chemicals and electrical impulses that combine with experience to make us the sentient beings that we are, does indeed have a soul, or spirit, that is central to existence. Somewhere between the neurological pathways, or perhaps as part of them, there is, I believe, an eternal soul, or spirit. I'm not sure where mind, body and soul/spirit begin and end; the borders between them seem more complicated to me now than when I was younger and knew so much more! However, I believe that mind-altering drugs can lower natural barriers in relation to areas of our self, allowing access to levels of consciousness that are normally dormant and perhaps best left that way.

Maybe it was early encounters with Christianity that gave me this perspective, but I felt a keen sense that I was touching something "other" in using drugs. I often entered visions with deep religious significance, and whilst my past occasional contact with church was with a Free Evangelical Church, with its distinct lack of emphasis on anything visual, impressionistic, iconic or symbolic, the visions that I had were generally the opposite. I would be out of my body, flying across great plains of crosses, moving inexorably towards those crosses that glowed golden in the distance. Or I would be in derelict Gothic church buildings where doves would flutter in the glimmering dust-motes of stained-glass windows. Or at times I passed beyond consciousness into a state of what seemed to me to be "universal oneness", each arm transformed in my mind into the spiral nebulae of uncreated stars forming in some distant galaxy! Aeons of time would pass in the quiet darkness that seemed completely integrated with my body and mind, planets drifting slowly through the silence of space as I watched with contented eyes.

I don't want to glamourize drug use, nor do I want to appear romantic or give an impression that I hold some kind of idyllic, nostalgic perspective about drugs. The stark reality is that I have seen too many friends die due to drug use, or to drug-related behaviours and accidents. However, for me there was a sense of spiritual quest and exploration in using them. At the end of the day, this was all happening during adolescence, which includes profound experiences of self-discovery, explorations of identity and growth across a number of psychological and physiological fronts – all enhanced and confused by a hormonal turmoil that is off the Richter Scale!

I believe that the combined forces of adolescence, drug use and the grace of God were eventually to lead me to the state of mind that would not tolerate half-truth, or the lure of a complacent submission to a world-view that was confined to the "here and now" or "the twin gods of intellect and reason". The questions had taken hold of me and I was seeking answers. I was knocking to open doors and asking for truth.

Some further thinking, reflection and stories

Many years later, after I had become a youth and community worker, I was faced with the question, "Can you dye a marijuana leaf into my hair, mate?"

I'd been face-painting and glass-painting at a Christian festival. I was amongst some of the young people on the fringe of things, when an eighteen-year-old levelled this question at me. I'd pitched my "detached youth work" stall (well, table!) outside of the disco. I could stand the bass notes of the dance music better from a small distance – must be my age! The lad who had approached me had been watching me paint with some of his mates. I guess he had decided that I had enough talent to attempt something to match the henna tattoo of the leaf that he had on his arm. He was slightly furtive with the question and seemed aware that he was testing a boundary of acceptability with me; one eye was on his mates as he waited for my reply.

I'd never dyed someone's hair – let alone dyed marijuana leaves! Dilemma: if I said yes, I was worried that I ran the risk of criticism from some of the Christian punters. If I said no, I ran the risk of alienating him, by my implied judgmental attitude. In the heat of the moment no neat third way occurred to me. There seemed no choice – pass the hair dye! Digging deep into my sixties psyche and glancing at his tattooed arm, I remembered the shape of the marijuana leaf and set to painting a full-scale version on the top of his head.

"Wicked, mate!" he said when he glanced at my efforts. He then put a £2 donation in the tin for street children.

With some distance from the event, I reflected and prayed over the experience. "Did I do right, Father?" Our conversation as I painted was interesting and seemed to justify my decision to some extent. I had used illegal drugs as I grew up (and still use legal ones such as tea, coffee and my ventolin inhaler to this day), so we chatted quietly about their use, the risks associated with different kinds of drugs and how to use them safely. This was a good piece of "harm reduction". However, what may have been more important was that we stayed in a non-judgmental relationship. We saw each other several times during the festival and shared a smile or greeting.

I wonder if this would have been the same had I said no.

I could tell that one or two of my Christian friends were less sure about my decision to try my hand at this kind of artistic pursuit! It's a tricky question for those working alongside young people. How do you stay in positive relationships with young people, being clear and open about your own values and beliefs, in ways that don't alienate or judge them? No easy answers will do: circumstances, conscience, experience, theology and our own unique perspectives will play their part in responding to the question in a multiplicity of ways. However, when I grapple with the question, my mind inevitably gravitates to the story of the woman caught in adultery. Jesus said to her, "Woman, where are they? Has no one condemned you?... Then neither do I condemn you... Go now and leave your life of sin." (John 8:10–11).

As a youth worker, I believe in the importance of harm-reduction in relation to young people and drug use. By engaging with this young person, I at least had an opportunity to discuss the implications of his interest in drugs. I try to alert and warn young people in an informed and non-judgmental way about drugs and the associated risks. I try to keep an open relationship with them, hopefully preventing them from doing harm to themselves or others. I have come across parents who mistrust their youngsters so much that they enter into a kind of "cops and robbers" relationship with them, to the extent that they are alienating themselves during a time when young people least need alienation from potentially helpful adults.

> *As a youth worker, I believe in the importance of harm-reduction in relation to young people and drug use.*

One parent visited my home on a Sunday morning to show me a screwed-up piece of paper containing some kind of black powder, which she had found in her son's pocket (which she regularly searched without his knowledge). She was worried that the paper contained drugs. I smiled as I realized what she was giving me and threw the little package across the room – where it exploded. It was a cracker! She was embarrassed at her naivety and we went on to have a good discussion about openness and trust, and how she might extract herself from the role of judge and jury over her son's lifestyle.

As a youth worker I think it is important to gather as much information about the impact of drugs as we possibly can so that we can share this in the conversations that we inevitably have with youngsters. We need to paint a realistic picture of drug use, not one that is based on the kind of grey-imaged advertising of the nineties that does not match the experience of most young people who do actually use drugs. We need to give them ideas about safe use rather than condemning their use. They need to know how to help themselves and their friends when things go wrong, and how to take action to prevent things going wrong in the first place.

I would apply the same argument to safe sex and young people. They need to be warned of the risks and they need access to contraception to avoid unwanted pregnancy or sexually transmitted diseases. This is not about condoning behaviour; it is about practical application of love in action, love that cares enough to respect young people and help them to make the best choices for themselves, even if they include choices that we don't approve of. I guess we all have memories we'd rather forget!

A few questions for your own reflection

- What are your "absolutes" in terms of values and beliefs in relation to any youth work practice you do?

- How do your own beliefs and ensuing behaviours affect your relationships with young people?

- Do you have a story of when you felt some conflict around values and beliefs?

- How do you "talk values and beliefs" in a non-threatening and appropriate way with young people? What methods, skills, principles and processes help in this area?

- What do you think of the "harm reduction" philosophy?

- What about promoting abstinence as an alternative (e.g. the Silver Ring movement from the USA that seeks to gain young people's commitment to no pre-marital sex)?

Story from the Edge 7:
Isla Horton

Sarah was nineteen when I first met her during some street work in 2002. She worked on the streets as a prostitute, used crack and heroin every day and lived alternately with punters and in squats. My colleague and I were walking the beat. We introduced Sarah to the outreach van and told her about the support available. From this point on Sarah began to use the van regularly and in December 2002 came into the project centre for the first time with a mate for our project Christmas dinner.

Over the next few months I saw Sarah irregularly during street outreach. At times she would talk, at other times she only wanted condoms, and was agitated waiting for the next punter to come along. Then Sarah completely disappeared from the street for three months. One night in June 2003, whilst out on foot, we came across Sarah again. She said she'd just come out of prison, had stopped using drugs while she was inside and really wanted to stay clean. "But how can I, when I just stick my head out the front door and three dealers come up to me?" She sobbed as she told us that she had started to use street drugs as soon as she came out of prison and · that her drug use had brought on seizures that she couldn't control. One night she had collapsed in the street and badly damaged her teeth. The one person she cared about was in prison for at least three years. She looked at us and said, "I want to die."

A few weeks later I saw Sarah again. This time she seemed much brighter and full of confidence. She was using drugs regularly again and

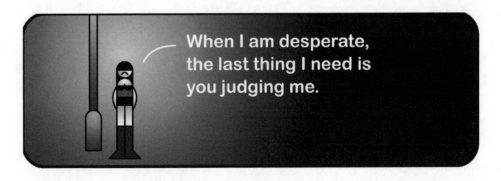

> When I am desperate, the last thing I need is you judging me.

showed no signs of wanting to stop. Two weeks on from this, we saw Sarah on the beat again. She said she didn't know what to do. She had discovered she had Hepatitis C. It was her two-year-old son's birthday tomorrow and she felt desperate. I arranged to meet Sarah to take her to a GP, but she never made the appointment. We continued to see Sarah on the van and out on foot for several weeks. Each time I offered to support her, she would agree to meet and then not show up.

Two weeks later I came into the office and a tired voice on the answer machine said, "Hi, it's Sarah. I'm in hospital. Can you come and visit me?" I went up to the ward armed with toiletries and chocolates, and we talked about what Sarah wanted to do, and what her options were. She had been admitted after a blood clot had formed in her leg. She had put off going to the doctor, until she had collapsed in pain. A day later in hospital, and Sarah would have lost her leg. She was scared and wanted to change. I talked her through her housing options and where she could get help with a methadone script, and I formed a loose action plan with her. She gave me a huge hug and said, "Thanks. You're a Godsend. I don't know where I'd be without the Project." I offered to pray for her, and then I left Sarah in the hospital, her future uncertain.

Three weeks later I bumped into Sarah one night on outreach. She didn't have much time to talk, but she did say, "Thank you. You really helped me." She was still homeless and injecting heroin into her groin again. Nothing, seemingly, had changed. The only difference was this – Sarah knew we were there for her. There was a connection now, and she knew that when she was ready for change, there would be someone there to walk alongside her as she took the first steps forward.

A few questions for your own reflection

- What has youth work got to offer people whose lives are as chaotic as Sarah's?

- What do you think about "harm reduction" in youth work?

- Would you give condoms to a young woman who is being abused through prostitution?

- How long do you keep going in youth work relationships?

- In this story, small steps have been made as the worker stays with the project. Where does this fit into the scheme of short-term funding programmes or career moves?

Story from the Edge 8:

Dave Wiles

"There's these three Scousers following me, mate! They've got knives and they've already stabbed other kids at the festival. They're after me next!"

I wasn't too surprised to be having this kind of conversation at the Glastonbury festival in the "Sanctuary Marquee" (run by Somerset Churches Together). That was why we were there – offering unconditional friendship, a listening ear and some basic human care for anyone who needed it. As I talked with Tom, it became apparent that this was not only a side-effect of drug-induced paranoia, but probably also an episode in his own delusional, phobic behaviour. As we chatted more, he mentioned the support he was getting from a psychiatric nurse. Whether or not the three Scousers existed was questionable. However, he was extremely worried and he was in a cold sweat, his eyes constantly scanning for trouble. He held on to me, fearing that I would leave him. Gradually I coaxed him to a social work service, and we were able to get him some appropriate help and support.

Of course, not all youth work activity will bring us into contact with mental health issues that are as sharp as Tom's were, but it is highly likely that our practice will mean that some of the young people we see have problems in this area of life. The Children's Society's *Good Childhood Report* (2009) indicates that 10 per cent of our young people suffer from some form of mental health problem. Studies of children aged between four and twenty suggest that diagnosable anxiety disorders affect around 12 per cent of this age group and disruptive disorders affect about 10 per cent of them (NCH Action for Children, *Fact File 2001*, p. 85).

In my experience I have worked with young people who demonstrate mildly distressing forms of anxiety, which can affect the way they relate to their peers and their view of themselves. I have also worked with young people whose behaviour has led to the need for serious medical intervention. There are a whole range of potential scenarios related to young people's mental and emotional well-being. For example, young people who "head bang" or self-harm, living out some terrible need to punish themselves or to draw attention to themselves; anorexic girls who are either passing through a phase of uncertain identity or dealing with some serious psychological problems; young Christians who read demonic activity into any troubled event in their lives; or compulsive behaviours; or obsessions; or over-dependence on drugs.

Of course, there are a number of potential roles for the youth worker in relation to mental health issues and young people, such as supporting and caring for them or advocating for appropriate services and ensuring that their voice is heard. We can also co-operate with and complement the work of other professionals, listen to young people, offer appropriate advice or help them to find it. Another key area is helping with relationships, and we have an unusual opportunity to ensure that young people who suffer from mental health issues are respected and included in group contexts in a non-patronizing and safe way. It's important to remember, as People First (a group who advocate with and for people who have learning disabilities) say, "Labels are for jars, not people!"

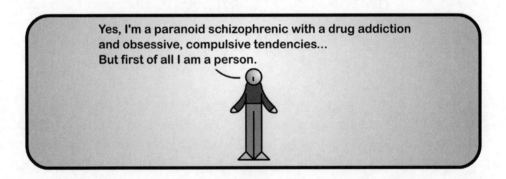

A complex area, which requires more consideration than I can give in this brief story, is the spiritual dimension of mental health issues. In my experience of youth work, I have come across two dangerous extremes. On one hand, there are those who don't recognize the spiritual dimension of the mind at all and are closed to the notion of prayer and sensitive spiritual responses. On the other hand, there are those who blunder in with ill-conceived spiritual explanations and remedial actions, which can end up causing all kinds of terrible harm. I tend to advocate a middle pathway that remains open to the power of prayer and understanding the spiritual dimension of our mental health, but which also draws upon the important lessons and insights that can be learnt from psychology and psychiatric professional colleagues.

A few questions for your own reflection

- This is an important topic for youth work (especially since the UK government's introduction of the Mental Health Bill 2006/07). What are your thoughts on youth work and its role in responding to mental health issues?

- Where do you stand in terms of your views about mental health and spirituality?

- How does your practice respond to the mental well-being of the young people that you come into contact with?

Story from the Edge 9:

Peter Hope

We were on our way back from the pub, returning to the residential Christian outdoor activity centre we were staying at. The staff, to their credit, came up to socialize with the group and everyone was in good spirits, England having just seen Turkey off in the European championship!

The evening had gone far better than I could have hoped. Taking a group of homeless young people from another area to my village local was, I pondered, a recipe for disaster. What would the church think? Would the youngsters get drunk or get into a fight? It's the scariest thing I have ever done as a youth worker. A mixed bunch of Christians and homeless people, we very conspicuous, with no corner to hide in!

> *It's the scariest thing I have ever done as a youth worker.*

It didn't start well. We walked in, and the whole pub froze to look at our motley congregation of bedraggled people. Gary the barman refused to serve Spangle; he even had his passport on him to prove he was twenty-one, although he only looked sixteen. Gary, now thirty, was a thirteen year old when he first came to our youth group, so I had a route in and he listened to my appeal and endorsement of Spangle's age. He agreed to serve him and ruffled feathers subsided, and the first hurdle was over. As the game kicked off, everyone was absorbed and concentrating on it.

I'll never forget that match; the atmosphere in the pub was electric. Turkey were all over us but when England scored the place erupted. I glanced round and everyone was hugging each other. Spangle was being embraced by a complete stranger, who previously had been eyeing him suspiciously, and two of the other lads were jumping up and down with a group of locals. In that moment of togetherness and equality, any sense of exclusion evaporated.

The game went on and England scored another goal. Conversations were now flowing and the good mood continued. Some of the locals took our group on at pool after the match. It was a great night of social interaction. Some might frown on our willingness to drink in the pub, and one of the group asked me if it was right for a Christian to drink alcohol at all. I replied that I was comfortable in the knowledge that Jesus ate and drank with many people and that it probably wasn't Perrier water he was drinking, and he probably wasn't in the company of the "right sort"! "Oh, what – you mean he would eat and drink with us, do you?"

We left the pub dead on closing time and on the way home Spangle asked me, referring to the centre we were staying at, "Why do they always say grace before meals?"

A valid enough question, which warranted a reply. "Well, it's to show God we're grateful for the food before us" was my rather standard and obvious reply.

> One thing is for sure – his gratitude for the little he got was real.

Spangle is a homeless young street lad who had been physically abused by his father – hence his preference for the street. His response left me humbled: "Listen, God knows how grateful I am for anything I get to eat, but I don't say grace coz he knows!"

I could have waffled on about meal-times being family times and a reminder that we are family, but his experience of family was a million miles from anything I had experienced. One thing is for sure – his gratitude for the little he got was real.

As we wandered home, under a wonderful canopy of stars, we talked about the game, the beer, the Centre we were staying at, and then Spangle floored me again by saying, "I wish I had family like them at the Centre."

We had a great weekend, unlikely as that was. They were a young, disaffected, marginalized adult group in strange surroundings, but amongst caring Christians who were real, and then amongst the secular pub community where, equally, there was acceptance of a sort. But the downside was that they had to go back to life on the streets, back into a twilight world of vulnerability – and there was nothing I could do to prevent that happening. That was the hardest thing. There was me, worrying about reputations, about whether everything would go off all right, hoping there wouldn't be any trouble – and they were returning to a lifestyle that was far more threatening and chaotic. I was left feeling superficial and inadequate. However, I resolved to continue the friendships that were formed during that weekend, when the saying of grace sparked a conversation that made me question myself beyond the knowledge of why we traditionally do things, in order to understand what saying grace is really all about.

A few questions for your own reflection

• How do you make connections with the existing spirituality of the young people that you come into contact with?

• What about some of the grey areas of morality that are important to some Christians and not so important to others?

• How do you cope with the criticism when it comes?

• How do you cope with the frustration of only chipping away at social problems [e.g. homelessness]?

• What can we do about the bigger picture?

Story from the Edge 10:

Isla Horton

I began working with Tracy just after she had been raped. The day after the attack she was out again working the beat. In a separate incident she was locked in a punter's flat and had to climb down a drainpipe to escape.

Tracy was just nineteen. She spent all day every day making money for her crack and heroin habits. We met over a fry-up in her B&B, then chatted as we walked along to the Sexual Health Centre where she was treated for several hours. After this Tracy came to the drop-in at our project several times a week. Usually she didn't want to talk to us. She just ate, crashed out on the sofa, and left. This continued for several months, with Tracy's health deteriorating rapidly. She was extremely underweight, dishevelled, sometimes incoherent and had lost her place at the B&B.

Then one week Tracy stopped coming in. She contacted me to say she was in prison and wanted support. I went to see her and supported her in court. As I liaised with probation, I advocated for Tracy to be given a place in a women's rehab outside of Bristol, the city we work in, and she was granted the place. After several months inside, on the day of her release Tracy was extremely emotional. "I want to stay clean and get my life back," she said over and over again.

Tracy had been estranged from her family since her brother's suicide a year earlier and was desperate to see them. I took her up to a Burger King for an emotional reunion. I wanted to help Tracy get away from the city and away from the drug scene she had been so deeply entrenched in. But after seeing her family, despite my strong advice to the contrary, Tracy insisted on being dropped off in the city to "say goodbye to her friends". Gutted, I went back to the project, thinking she wouldn't make it that day.

Late that afternoon the door-bell rang and Tracy came into the drop-in in tears. "All my friends wanted me for was my drugs. All my stuff's gone. My boyfriend's with some other girl. I haven't got anything left." Finally, when she knew for herself that she had nothing to hold onto, Tracy wanted to catch the train to the women's rehab. It wasn't too late. We raced to the station and I sat waiting for the train to pull away. I had taken her as far as I could.

From this point I wrote to Tracy every so often and supported her in her updates in court. I hadn't heard from Tracy for six months when she phoned to say that she'd been kicked out of rehab and was coming back to Bristol. She was still drug free but needed to be in a rehab straight away. A new home for women recovering from drugs and prostitution had just opened. I referred Tracy in and she continued to work at her recovery.

As I write, Tracy is almost one year clean from using any drugs and working the street. She is barely recognizable as the girl I met over the fry-up. She has created her own support network, and we still meet every so often for coffee. Tracy was very keen to help other young people who were struggling, so I helped her find a place to volunteer. She now uses her wonderful art skills and her life experience to help other vulnerable young people in a local project.

A few questions for your own reflection

- How do you get the balance between helping young people in the circumstances they are in, whilst wanting better things for them and trying to move them on?

- How do you form relationships wherein you can challenge young people's current views and beliefs without alienating them from your friendship and support?

- How do you retain contact with young people when they move on or have a chaotic lifestyle?

Chapter 3

Conversion, Comfort and Risk

Many years ago, when I worked as a volunteer at a hospital, I got to know a little girl named Liz who was suffering from a rare and serious disease. Her only chance of recovery appeared to be a blood transfusion from her five-year-old brother, who had miraculously survived the same disease and had developed the antibodies needed to combat the illness. The doctor explained the situation to her young brother, and asked the little boy if he would be willing to give his blood to his sister. I saw him hesitate for only a moment before taking a deep breath and saying, "Yes, I'll do it if it will save her." As the transfusion progressed, he lay in bed next to his sister and smiled, as we all did, seeing the colour returning to her cheek. Then his face grew pale and his smile faded. He looked up at the doctor and asked with a trembling voice, "Will I start to die right away?" Being young, the little boy had misunderstood the doctor; he thought he was going to have to give his sister all of his blood in order to save her.

Source unknown

I walked out of the pub in my element! Two girlfriends were with me and the alcohol and dope had worked their confidence-giving effect. Even though the pubs were closing we had the clubs to hit, and the night was young. That was when we met Ed, whom the girls knew, and of whom I was deeply suspicious. After all, anyone who had a "Honk if you love Jesus" sticker on their car had to be a sandwich short of a full picnic, in my opinion!

Ed was driving a three-wheeled car for disabled people; he was a Jesus freak with hair and beard to match those of his guru! Ed had cerebral palsy and the dubious (and very un-PC) nickname of "the Crippy Hippy" – he was an ex-hippy who used to smuggle drugs around in his crutches. He was gently spoken and had just come out of the local Christian youth café, which was called "Four Square". Square indeed, I thought!

However, he was a great conversationalist and I was soon drawn into a discussion about a Christian crusade that was taking place in the city, and before I knew it, I had accepted a leaflet inviting me to go along and find out "The Way To Life". I stuffed the leaflet in my back pocket and thought I might use it as a roach when rolling a joint later that night. A crusade was the last thing I needed. I wondered if Richard the Lionheart might attend.

Growing convictions

As the weekend wore on, I began to wonder about Christianity again. What if all they had taught me at Sunday school was true? Was there a God? What happens when you die? Who was Jesus and was it possible to have a personal relationship with him? Of course, these are questions that are common to many in adolescence. However, they were revisiting me with a vengeance, and I have to confess to a sense of desperation.

I half decided to check out the crusade and took the three-mile walk into town, wondering whether to follow through this instinct or head for the pub. I wandered into the crusade. The singing had already begun and it wasn't long before I wondered what on earth I had done. Happy-clappy, well-dressed people who seemed to be enthusiastic about God rather than scared of him, as I was. However, the truth is that I was probably not brave enough to walk out of the meeting, even though I was sitting at the back of the massive crowd.

Then the preacher took the rostrum and started to tell the story of Zacchaeus from the Bible. Of course, I identified strongly with this little character; I had sneaked up on the crowd to give Jesus a viewing. My life was certainly up a gum tree and I was well enough aware of my own "short" comings! As I listened, it was as if I had got into a one-on-one conversation with God. My questions were being responded to, my image of God was being reframed from one of a celestial spoilsport, who wreaked vengeance on anyone whom he suspected of having a good time, to that of a loving Father who had been willing to send his only Son to die for me.

> *As I listened, it was as if I had got into a one-on-one conversation with God.*

I was experiencing a sense of euphoria and wonder, and as the preacher gave the altar call, I rushed out to respond to this scandalous story of amazing grace. The hymn they were singing was "Just as I am, without one plea... O Lamb of God I come", and whilst I didn't have a clue about what the biblical imagery meant, I was sure that I needed this Jesus they were singing about.

The "follow-up counsellor" who I was linked up with after the crusade did a great job of taking me through the spiritually correct procedures of salvation. However, I was already on fire with God – all lit up inside with a sense of everlasting life! The experience that I had of freedom and liberation was overwhelming and I delighted in a transcendent feeling of homecoming. It was as if I was becoming who I was meant to be; it all seemed to fall into place. As Eugene Peterson puts it in *The Message*, I was becoming my "true child-of-God [self]" (John 1:12). I hadn't read the words of Jesus, "the water I give will become in him a spring of water welling up to eternal life" (John 4:14), but that was exactly my experience. The parched and barren landscape of my life was flooded with a sense of peace and joy.

Into the "Total Perspective Vortex"[3]

I walked home in a state of bliss that was to last for the next year or so. Everything seemed different, the landscape was more vibrant with colour and life, and somehow people seemed more important to me. Indeed, one of my first actions as a Christian was to anonymously pay back the old couple I had robbed earlier that month to sustain my drink and drug habits. I didn't have the courage to apologise to them openly; I hoped they would understand that I was sorry.

I started to give money to charities instead of stealing their collecting boxes, as I had done in the past. I developed a new sensitivity to others. Instead of my normal headlong pursuit of self-gratification, I started to dig old people's gardens for them, without any payment.

I returned a photograph that I had stolen on the last day at my old school and apologised to teachers for the way that I had treated them when I was at school. I was very pleasantly surprised when later one of the teachers gave me back the same picture that I had stolen! It was five years after I had returned it, and on his retirement he decided to give it to me as a way of thanking me for my honesty!

My Mum and Dad were a bit shocked by the changes, to say the least, and they put it down to a "phase" of my life. However, I know that they both watched me carefully over the years, and I later discovered that they too had responded to an appeal during a Billy Graham rally in the 1950s, and they saw my conversion as a reminder of that commitment.

As I have mentioned, during my first year as a Christian, I seemed to be on a new plane of existence. Everything seemed to fall into place for me; I had a job on a building-site and found the banter over my new-found faith quite stimulating. I confess, though, that at times I got a bit judgmental and depressed about the language on the site and the arguments that I had with some of the men.

It got so bad that on one occasion I gave in my notice. The Welsh foreman looked at me as I handed in my resignation and commented that this wasn't something that my Master would do! I am so grateful for his wisdom. Whether it was inspired by a background in chapel or prompted by God, I don't know, but for me it was a reminder that faith is not about looking for easy options and that "comfortable Christianity" is an oxymoron.

I withdrew my notice, swallowed my pride and tried to love the men I worked with in the way that I knew Christ did. The results were stunning. I had endless individual in-depth conversations with most of the men about life, the universe and everything! I was learning the valuable lesson that the way people react in a group is so different from what they are really like.

After a year or so as a Christian I was also wondering about my former friends – those who haunted the bars, clubs and discos in the centre of the city. They must have wondered where I had got to. I had a growing sense

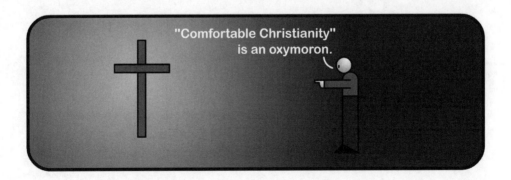

of unease about my now hermit-like existence which consisted of work, reading my Bible, prayer and church. One evening, as I was walking to the church youth group, my conscience pricked me over the way I had deserted my former friends in the city. Wasn't the good news relevant to them too? Wasn't God interested in those outside of the church?

I faced a dilemma. There was this growing unease that God was interested in my friends and that perhaps he wanted me to reconnect my story to theirs. On the other hand, there was the unspoken fear that if I went back to the highways and byways of my former life, my new Christian friends would use that dreaded phrase – "backsliding"! Perhaps they would think that I was back on drugs or the bottle, or worse still, that I was perhaps going to a different church! It makes me smile, looking back, but at the time it felt like a life-threatening decision: "Do I go back to my city friends or do I stay at the youth group?" I confess that the decision was so overwhelming that I resorted to flipping open the Bible for some guidance – not a method I would necessarily advocate, but one that I turned to then in simplicity and sincerity.

I left the rest of the young people to their table-tennis and table-football and crept into the back room of the church. In the dying daylight I stood before the church Bible. It was an imposing book, but one that I was beginning to love and respect and which I was trying to read in the right way. However, on this occasion I wasn't looking for theological correctness. I needed a clear understanding. What should I do next? I flipped its pages open and read the first verse that my eyes alighted on: "Make haste now, for he came today to the city" (1 Samuel 9:12, KJV). This seemed fairly clear to me! So I left the church that very evening, walked into the city and reconnected with my friends. And many adventures followed.

Perhaps faith is spelt "R-I-S-K"

These kinds of experiences don't happen to me often, but when they do, they go deep. It was the beginning of a theme that continues in my own spiritual journey; an experience which has underlined for me the centrality of seeking

to include as many as possible in the good news of forgiveness, acceptance and love; to promote an inclusive kingdom that welcomes one and all, and especially those who are often left out. I believe that the church needs to be ready to go to where people are instead of asking them to come. I've often said that "gospel" has "go" as its first two letters. It's not a "comespel"!

Faith should be spelt "R-I-S-K". What is it that turns Christianity (in the West) into such a tame and safe expression of what should be the most radical and revolutionary lifestyle ever imagined? How do we get seduced into conformity with values and ideals that seem a million miles from those expressed by Jesus? What turns his revolution into something that can be contained within ceremonies, liturgies and behaviours that have so little impact on the real issues around us? We have been sleep-walking into a world-view that allows us to tolerate crass comments from each other about church such as, "I didn't get much out of the worship today" – comments that are laced with consumerist ideals that have forced us to forget that worship is costly and that service is central to it (e.g. see Romans 12). God is not another commodity on the shelf of postmodern choice. Why invest in better incomes, bigger houses and larger cars? It all turns to dust! Why not invest in the things that have lasting value – in people, in each other and in the kingdom of God? I have found time and time again, in my faith journey, that life in all its fullness and adventures aplenty wait for me when I turn from my obsession with self, when I learn again what it is to follow Jesus, instead of just talking about him.

Begin to express your faith where you are

As a new Christian I was concerned about young people and children, and one of the things I began to do was to help run Christian activities on a council estate that adjoined the one where I lived. There was no church on the estate and we decided to open one for children and young people in the local youth club. Each week we had up to a 150 youngsters between six and sixteen joining us for games, songs, quizzes and Bible stories. It was a form of emergent youth and children's church long before such terms became fashionable. On one occasion I asked the children and young people if they had Bibles and discovered that many didn't have one. Despite being unemployed at the time, I decided to practise risky faith and told them that if God gave me the money, I would buy one for everyone who wanted one. Surprise, surprise – the cheque came the next day! It was money that the court fines system owed me from a young man who had finally paid off his fine for stealing a scooter of mine several years before. I took it that this was God's provision (it was the *justice* system!) and spent all the money on twenty-four Bibles. The children and young people were thrilled when I told them that God had provided for us. I was doubly thrilled when no more and no less than twenty-four youngsters came to claim a Bible after the meeting!

I have to confess that I am not so sure that my faith today is always as "red blooded" as it was back then. However, it seems to me that we do well to observe the tortoise – who gets nowhere unless he sticks his neck out!

Some further thinking, reflection and stories

This chapter has touched on my own conversion story and the evolving nature of faith development and risk taking. The stories that follow touch on these themes from a number of differing perspectives. Christian youth and community work, by its nature, is in the arena of spiritual development – a tricky area that has some people reaching for their Bibles and some reaching for the bucket! I would like to offer a few thoughts that I consider important in terms of how we express responsibility in working in this arena.

The Message

Liberation theologians argue that the "message" of Christianity is critical and that the "models" of being a Christian are far less important. Marins, Trevisan and Chanona offer the following parable to illuminate the difference between "message" and "model":

> *It was the day of festivities – a day of music, colour, bustling crowds and above all joy. One person in particular had to be there – the man who sold the multi-coloured balloons and who was always the delight of the children and the adults. A little black boy, with all the innocence of a four year old, came up to him and asked, "If you had a black balloon would it also go up?" The balloon seller replied, "Of course son. What makes the balloon go up is the air inside, not the colour."*[4]

The danger with much Christian activity is that we spend time and energy propagating the "models" of Christianity that we have developed instead of remaining faithful to the sharing of the "message". We are often preoccupied with the colour of the balloon rather than the air that fills it. In Christian youth work, in many cases, a host of subliminal and hidden conditions are conveyed through insinuation and subtle approval/disapproval to young people as to what Christianity is and how it should be practised.

I have often used a role-play exercise[5] with youth workers and church leaders to explore this phenomenon. The role play involves groups of people exploring scriptures to identify the role and developmental patterns of a number of early churches (Antioch, Jerusalem, Rome etc.). The groups explore significant events in the development of those churches, key individuals in their story and the values, theology and beliefs that are core to their identity. After this process the groups are asked to role play the early church that they have studied and they are then asked to "visit" each other, in role, to share something of their history and traditions, to tell a story that is significant in their community, and also to exchange a gift.

At times the results have been both profound and extremely funny. They have illustrated well the depth of discord and dissonance between evolving models of church in the early church. For example, in one group that I worked with, the Corinthians took a bacon sandwich as their gift to the church at Jerusalem. Hardly kosher!

One of the interesting outcomes of the exercise has been the obvious tensions and potential divisions that have come to the surface in the role play, as groups have engaged in dialogue and explored their core beliefs in role. Some of the key learning points that I have identified from the exercise are:

- The message of the gospel impacted cultures in the early church in very different ways. The context and culture in which the message was "released" is a key factor in how the model of church evolved.

- The role play brings to the surface differences and disagreements that were very real for the early church. These often became a source of tension and division. Looked at from a more distant perspective, ensuing schisms could have been avoided if the concept of "win-win" was embraced, especially if differing groups had realized that they each had valid perspectives.

- The early church groups each had special and precious traditions, experiences and events that shaped who they were. These were held on to as "formative characteristics" which, whilst of great significance to the group, were not a common experience or easily understood by others.

The parallels to our own contemporary experience of church are always clear to those engaging in the exercise. The depth of discussion regarding the impact that this must have on those outside of the church, particularly young people, is always salutary. Liberationists would argue that our fidelity should always be to the message of Christianity and not to the models of church that have evolved around it. Of course, this then opens up the discussion, "Well, what *is* the message?" Perhaps you would like to stop reading for a while and explore your own understanding of the message.

What exactly is the message, then?

This brief exercise is designed to help you explore what you think of as central to the Christian message. Read the statements below, which have been produced by a number of my own youth worker contacts who were asked to "define the Christian message/gospel in up to fifteen words... in the essence of what it means to you". Explore which of the statements resonate with your own understanding of the message. Why is this? What are these statements saying about the message? What is central to the message? What is non-negotiable? How would you use fifteen words to come up with the heart of the Christian message for yourself? Below is a sample of the responses that I received from over a hundred youth workers:

- It changes everything. I now know love, I have purpose. I have hope.

- We are all bastards but God loves us anyway.

- God was in Christ reconciling the world to himself.

- Jesus loves me – this I know, for the Bible tells me so.

- The gospel provides a good framework and set of rules which I aspire to.

- Thou shalt love the Lord thy God... and thy neighbour as thyself.

- New life through Jesus from the perfect Father, guided and safe – forever.

- Freedom, forgiveness, love and hope – that's what Jesus gives when we ask him inside!

- God is love and loves to give good things; he gave his best present – Jesus.

- Love, love, love, love, love, love, love, love, love, love, love, love, love, love, love!

- Good news for the poor, justice and shalom, the kingdom come, now and not yet.

- Christianity gives me a sense of purpose, of belonging and a reason for life.

- Hope. The promise of a happy ending where glorifying God is my only mission.

- This is a wonderful world made by God, screwed up by people, but redeemed by Christ.

- The unknown, but strangely familiar person travelling the journey with me.

- God + man + sin = separation. Jesus + crucifixion + sin = death. Jesus + death = resurrection! Resurrection = man − sin.

- For me the Christian faith comes down to three words. Grace through Christ.

- COMMUNITY!!!

- Our only hope on the shoulders of a carpenter on a cross, our God, Jesus.

- The King of the universe, held vulnerable in the gentle arms of a young mum.

- God loves you and me. Passionately, recklessly. Such love demands a response – your whole life!

- Love, forgiveness, friendship, community, hope, fresh start/new life, freedom, power, knowing God, eternal, truth.

- Jesus is Lord – you must choose to follow him or reject him.

- God's love can transform the worst person, if you are willing to let him.

My own understanding of the Christian message would place emphasis on the centrality of grace. Put simply, it seems to me that a unique factor of Christianity is the belief in a God who has not only created humanity, and defined what is good for us as individuals and communities (the law), but has also redeemed us by becoming one of us (in Christ) and offering himself as the means of grace and forgiveness for the whole of humanity. Our part of the process is to accept this grace through penitence and belief. In my experience this has been paradoxically both a single event and an ongoing process. Philip Yancey revels in the wonder of God's grace, in that God chooses to partner with the frailty of humanity:

> *Why would God choose Jacob the conniver over dutiful Esau? Why confer supernatural powers of strength on a delinquent named Samson? Why groom a runty shepherd boy, David, to be Israel's king? And why bestow a sublime gift of wisdom on Solomon, the fruit of that king's adulterous liaison? Indeed, in each of these Old Testament stories the scandal of grace rumbles under the surface until finally, in Jesus' parables, it bursts forth in a dramatic upheaval to reshape the moral landscape.[6]*

However, before you accept my particular rendition of the "good news", perhaps a note of caution is worth consideration. I rather suspect that the good news is less about some codex of linguistic correctness and more about what has happened to you and I in our encounters with the grace and love of God. It is rooted in how we find the gentle, respectful and humble ways of giving account of the hope that is in us, with a clear conscience, to those we come into contact with (see 1 Peter 3:15).

A subjective but sensitive and appropriate sharing of our own personal "love story" is likely to be heard more deeply than the ranting of insecure dogmatists. Authentic encounters that are rooted in mutual learning and respect seem so much more Christ-like than those that want to indoctrinate others, often out of a sense of their own insecurity.

Listening to the still small voice of someone else's doubts and tentative leanings to faith resonates with the voice of God, for me, far more than the programmed spiritual pap and certainty that some seek to force-feed to young people. I think that spirituality that starts with people's experience, rather than the particular theological obsessions of

> *A subjective but sensitive and appropriate sharing of our own personal "love story" is likely to be heard more deeply than the ranting of insecure dogmatists.*

extremists, reaches the soul far more readily.

I believe that, to many people, Christianity is an unhelpful mystery. We can unpack that mystery for them if we are willing to share our personal spiritual stories at the right time.

Christian baggage has to go!

The reshaping of the moral landscape that Yancey writes about is what excites me about Christianity. One of the most outrageous characteristics of grace seems to me to be that it is totally outside of conditions – a factor which seemed to disturb the religious leaders of Jesus' times (see Matthew 12:1–3, 9–10; 15:1–9; 16:1–4 etc.) and, I believe, many in our own times. Christianity is too often laden with baggage, most of which relates to the models of church that have evolved after the message has been released into a particular culture or context.

I would want to question much of the baggage that churches seem to want to load onto young people, if they are to become Christians. This kind of baggage is not always a considered or conscious message that the church gives to young people. However, the unwritten collective assumptions in many churches about what being a Christian constitutes prevent many young people from even tentatively considering the Christian faith. Many of the youngsters I have known would not even give Christianity a second glance, on the basis that they believe they could never be good enough to be a Christian. They need to know that Christianity is not so much a fixed destination as a choice to make a journey. Whilst we are busy defining faith as a fixed location, we run the risk of seduction to the security of vain tradition.

Where has this misunderstanding that Christians are good come from? Has Christianity become a sanctimonious, self-righteous hobby, no better than the religious experience of the Pharisees and Sadducees of Jesus' times? A hobby that has replaced a poignant and humbling knowledge of the fact that we are forgiven humans, relating to a gracious God through his own costly sacrifice. Black-and-white judgmental morality is in danger of replacing empathetic understanding of others – a kind of comfortably numb

Christianity that has no time for a theology of grace and ongoing salvation.

Vincent Donavan expresses well the kind of approach that I believe young people need from youth workers in relation to the development and nourishment of a shared spiritual journey:

> *In working with young people do not try to call back to where they were and do not call them to where you are, as beautiful a place as that may seem to you. You must have the courage to go with them to a place that neither you nor they have ever been before.*[7]

The skills that I think are critical for this kind of activity include:

- An ability to review and reflect on shared experience. It is much easier to have a prepared, packaged view of spirituality that can be dispensed in spoonfuls of "received wisdom" than it is to stay with an honest question about the road ahead. An open mind and heart will help, and there must be a willingness to utter the dreaded phrase, "I don't know" from time to time! This skill is about the ability to conduct intentional reflection. Whilst often frowned upon by those with more didactic inclinations, it is a skill that can facilitate deep and meaningful learning and change.

- An ability to organize and facilitate processes that young people can enjoy together and can go deeper with, in terms of inner exploration and some good group work skills. It's really important to remember that we all learn in differing ways and to connect with learning styles in a way that enables mutual learning and discovery.

- Communication skills are obviously necessary. Listening as well as speaking goes without saying. It will be critically important to be able to summarize and ask open questions. Be sensitive to the group's mood, and from time to time offer theoretical and/or theological inputs in a way that young people can relate to. It will also be important to know when to stay silent!

A few questions for your own reflection

- What is your message? How would you share the hope that you have within you? What are the conditions for sharing the message - for example, in terms of the settings, situations and circumstances in which you think it appropriate to share your story?

- Are there particular factors that you think are important in relation to faith and spiritual development when considering it with children and young people? What kind of guidelines would you have? Have you had any good/bad experiences of this in observing others? What did you learn from them?

- How has your own experience of church impacted the way that you understand spiritual development amongst children and young people? How has "church" helped/hindered this theme for you and the children and young people you work with?

- I have suggested that faith should be spelt "R-I-S-K" in this chapter. What do you think about that? How does it make you feel and why do you think you feel that way? How much risk is there in your experience of faith? Are you comfortable with that? Is there a theological imperative to taking risks in our faith? If so, what scriptures, stories and perspectives support or inform this?

Story from the Edge 11:
Dave Wiles

I'm fresh (if that's the right word!) back from the Glastonbury festival and have been reflecting on the work that Frontier Youth Trust has been involved with in the Sanctuary Marquee at the festival, which is organized by Somerset Churches Together. We are there, as part of the Christian church, to "demonstrate the love of Christ in action by offering festival-goers a warm welcome, space to reflect and a willingness to listen". On the ground (or should I say in the mud!) this includes: providing somewhere for up to 140 people to sleep when they have lost their tent/faculties; giving out 10,000 cups of water to potentially dehydrated passers-by; watching over someone who has crashed on drugs or drink; listening and laughing with festival-goers; painting faces; playing games; making banners; praying with someone who wants to reconnect with God... We had seventy volunteers providing 24-hour-a-day cover throughout the festival in the name of Christ.

We adopted a theme at the festival this year "Who are you?" – and reinforced it by getting people to paint portraits of each other, by banner making and by playing around with some huge mirrors (the giant kaleidoscope was particularly popular!) I was struck by the significance of this simple theme/message and was reminded of how central it is to quality relational youth work. It was great to be alongside people in an unconditional way, to experience the power of "open voluntary relationships" that led into some amazing conversations about life, the universe and everything. So many encounters stand out in my mind, as I remember people coming to check out why we were providing this service to the festival. We had all agreed that it was a "no-preach zone". However, the God conversations were plentiful and very authentic. "I can't cope with church, but if it was like this – wow!" someone said as they encountered the Sanctuary. All too often other agendas dominate our youth work: numbers for the funding applications; conversions to keep the "elders" happy; education and employment to keep the government on board; or "journal fodder" for the latest youth work training you signed up for. It's easy to lose sight of the power of just being with young people, and taking time to ask, "Who are you?"

I was at Glastonbury during the close of an "urban pilgrimage" that Tim Evans (CEO of Worth Unlimited) and I had just completed. We wandered around three urban areas, asking young people if God could be found anywhere and, if God could be found, where would he be? I thought you might be interested in some of the responses we had to a text-message service that we established for young people to write to God as part of the pilgrimage learning. The messages seem to reinforce the importance of relational youth work that "fleshes out" something of God's heart for young people:

> *Are you rich? Are you white? Fanxs for everyfin but y is the world so cruel. I no that its becoz we will then appreciate the good fings but what's da point? Do you forgive? When will I die? Dear God if you are real give me a sign so I can believe. Where are you when I need you most? I think I might be gay – Is this bad? I hope you know how much I love and appreciate u. We don't talk very much and that's my fault – can we have a heart to heart soon, thanks.*

I offer these thoughts from Glastonbury, and some of the voices from the pilgrimage, as a word of encouragement to those youth workers who are still helping young people to find something of a relationship with God by making the time and space to bother with finding out who young people are. Perhaps those beautiful feet that bring good news wear muddy wellies!

A few questions for your own reflection

- How are you getting on in terms of relational youth work - has someone else's agenda taken over or started to influence you?

- Are you able to listen effectively to young people?

- How do you do it, and if you had to advise someone else on the value of it and how to go about it, what would you say?

Story from the Edge 12:

Chris Bristow

At a recent youth project meeting we shared the story of a fifteen-year-old young man who was having a very difficult time in his life. He was so obviously at a crossroads where he had serious problems at home and was flirting with a peer group who were into all kinds of negative and destructive behaviour. But he was wanting and needing support from others in the neighbourhood to divert him away from this lure of crime and deviance. There was a window of opportunity to help. Someone in our group had two free tickets to a theme park and so a day out was planned for him, two others and two volunteer youth workers. Good friendships were made and they met regularly for a few months. He's now moved on to other things and, we hope, to many more positive experiences.

How can we measure a friendship? What is the value of shared thoughts and tears? In a small way we were able to recognize this window opening, but most of us seldom have time to stop and change our direction in life's hectic journey. Jesus had time, took time and made time to be with others and with his Father. So much of what we do in youth work today is measured by systems of evaluation and performance review which run the risk of being preoccupied with "hard data" and high numbers. You wonder if Jesus would have been allowed to visit the woman at the well in Samaria, as it wasn't "value for money" or an "economic use of his time" or statistically correct! I'm not undermining the need for monitoring and evaluation; I'm just wanting to apply a reasonable health warning to what might be driving our practice. Perhaps the question is, how do we develop systems that respect the quality of what we do as well as the quantity?

Peter Brierley underlines some of the contradictions for young people growing up today. He says our current generation of young people (GenXers) are

> *the first electronic generation, with the ability to process lots of information simultaneously; the first generation to be raised completely by TV and shaped by music... needing the church more than any other generation and wanting it so little.*

> **Church of England Newspaper, 8 June 2001**

The potential for quality time being shared between individual adults and young people runs the risk of being squeezed out by the frenzied nature of society. How does church and youth work slow down enough to reconnect with young people through safe, authentic and committed relationships? Perhaps we should add this to the parable about the sheep and the goats in Matthew 25:31–46: "When I needed you, you were there; when I wanted your time, you gave it; when I barely had time to listen to myself, you heard me."

A few questions for your own reflection

- Are you and your church aware of or close enough to such young people?

- When was the last time you had space enough to recognize and respond to such a need?

- Are there "windows" in your schedule to respond in the way that occurred in this story?

- How and where does your church [i.e. the gathering of people who say that they follow Christ] follow Christ in this way?

- Isn't church sometimes too self-centred and interested in itself and its members to be able to respond to others?

- Why do we insist on creating such a self-centred existence when it comes to being church [i.e. a worshipping community]?

- What do we need to change and how can you change?

- Are you able to give time to these questions, even? What are the dangers? What are the potential excuses?

Story from the Edge 13:

Dave Wiles

"I woke in the middle of the night, I needed some whiz and I knew where I could get some. Then I remembered that you had said that one of the ways I could cope with drugs was to pray."

This was the way the conversation with Carl was going a few years ago. I was on the edge of my chair, wondering if he had prayed – he had! As he had lain in bed he had tentatively whispered the Lord's Prayer.

"Then what happened?" I asked.

"Oh, nothing – I just fell asleep!"

Carl and I had probably expected a "wham"-type deliverance from drugs as the answer to his prayer. However, while we mulled it over as we drank our coffee, we both realized that we had to leave it with God to answer the prayer as he saw fit.

Carl was eighteen. I'd known him since he was about seven, and even then he had demonstrated addictive behaviours. He was petrol- and glue-sniffing before he'd reached double years. Later on, during that week of his prayer, he became a Christian. Things changed slowly; however, he never made the transition to formal church. We stayed in touch until, some years later, I heard that he had died, having drifted back into the drug scene.

God, it hurt! His wife and two children were devastated, even though he had left them for a life on the road some time ago. I keep coming back to questions about the way in which Carl could never integrate with other Christians in a formal church context. We met and occasionally prayed together and I know that he had a deep faith. However, it was one he could never seem to work out in the formal church context with other believers. How can we be more open and inclusive in our churches?

In the various church-based talks that I do for FYT, I often say that I spend half my time with people outside of the church trying to convince them to come in and the other half of my time with people inside the

> *I often say that I spend half my time with people outside of the church trying to convince them to come in and the other half of my time with people inside the church telling them to get out!*

church telling them to get out! It's a real challenge for Christians to stay open to all and to break down the barriers that can keep particular groups out.

One very real encouragement for me is the story of Aunt Dorothy (an eighty-plus-year-old saint who is now with her Lord in glory). She had a real heart for marginalized and excluded young people – however, she once confessed to me that she sometimes found gangs of ten or so leather-clad young people a bit intimidating!

Dorothy went on to say how she overcame her fear by using her "little lost old lady" routine. Despite her intimate knowledge of the city she lived in, she would often approach groups of young people and ask for directions. She found that this was a way of starting conversations which helped her overcome her own fear and often led to in-depth relationships with many young people who, like me, came to know and love her as "Aunt Dorothy".

Dorothy found that her vulnerability was something that young people responded to with care and concern – contrary to much popular belief. Interestingly, she would often be seen the day after she had approached a group, taking several of them to church!

My reflections on Carl's life and death and Aunt Dorothy's mission to the marginalized lead me to several questions:

A few questions for your own reflection

- Did I do enough to help Carl?

- Do we do enough to help the many other young people like Carl who are outside of so much church-based youth work?

- If there was some alternative form of church, would/could he have become part of a healing community?

- What do you think of "youth churches"?

- How do we enable both young people and older church-folk to find enough common ground to listen to each other and get beyond the stereotypes?

Story from the Edge 14:

Peter Hope

Kelly claimed that her life was an accident, and from an early age she struggled to believe that she was accepted and loved, even though she came from a settled home with caring parents.

At school life was hard. She was often bullied and she under-achieved. As she grew she yearned to be accepted and learnt that if she was free with her favours to the boys, they, at least, seemed to offer her some temporary protection from the bullies who plagued her life. But she gained a reputation as an easy lay and encountered further abuse.

She left school at fifteen without a single qualification, started to drift around from one temporary job to another, and in a desperate attempt to make something of her life, moved to the east coast to a holiday centre to try to find work in entertainment, as she enjoyed singing. But unscrupulous men preying on her vulnerability took advantage of her. She returned to her parents' home, deflated and depressed.

She was now eighteen and at this point her life took a turn for the worse. She was raped by a 48-year-old man whom she was helping at a karaoke evening. There had been several incidents, and at first she was frightened for her own safety. When she did turn for help, nobody believed her because of her reputation, and his fervent denials.

Her life now spiralled downwards. Her already burgeoning eating disorder developed quickly. Rapidly losing weight and self-harming, she disengaged from her family and left the area, becoming homeless. Finally, she made a serious attempt to end her life.

It was at this point that she was committed to a rehabilitation unit, and the slow and tortuous road to some form of recovery began. She received medical attention, counselling and treatment, eventually returning to the area she had fled from. She was re-housed by a Christian housing trust.

She now has regular daily support as an outpatient at a local unit specializing in the treatment of eating disorders and depression. She also receives support via a housing worker. It is intensive work for all those connected to her, striving to resettle Kelly back into independent living, working to restore her self-esteem and confidence, and repairing broken family ties.

Alcoholics, drug users and self-harmers seem intent on damaging themselves, knowing full well the consequences of their behaviour and the effect it has on those around them. Nothing seems to arrest their actions. Imminent death is not a deterrent when life holds nothing but dread.

Kelly's life is slowly on the mend, but she is permanently scarred, physically and emotionally. She needs a lot of attention and support. It's demanding work, but at least she is getting the help she needs. How many other Kellys are there – vulnerable, abused, a statistic waiting to be recorded – slipping through the net into self-induced oblivion?

A few questions for your own reflection

- How can we communicate a message of hope and confidence, which will penetrate into their world of despair and fear?

- How can we, in our role as youth workers, be involved in enabling young people to see themselves differently, to maybe get in touch with a more positive and loving image of themselves?

- What are the skills and processes that we should be developing to help people like Kelly?

Story from the Edge 15:
Bev Palmer

I had been a schools youth worker and counsellor for two years when I first met Laura. She was a pretty, headstrong, streetwise thirteen-year-old. She came on the pretext of helping a "friend" who thought she might be pregnant. I gave contact numbers but said that I would be available for support if it was needed. She came back, but this time she was more honest – she was the one who needed help!

This was where our relationship began. I mediated for her with family, school and the medical services and became a sounding-board for all her fears and concerns. I was amazed at her ability to survive the massive changes that came her way. I was proud of her, charmed by her and wanted nothing but the best for her. I also believed in her. Her little girl was born and it was then she shared her greatest fear: "What if history repeats itself?" Both her grandma and her mum had had babies in their teens.

I continued working with Laura and supporting her through all the twists and turns of her life. I was continually reminded throughout that working with young people cannot be done without a profound sense of hope, particularly when you find yourself exposed to the often raw but real situations and emotions experienced by them. The tension rests not only in accompanying them on their life's journey, but knowing how to reflect and communicate a sense of hope. Especially into lives and circumstances that appear hopeless situations that often result in an incredible loss of potential.

Searching together for hope in a sea of hopelessness feels hopeless, but at least we have each other.

It was not that Laura did not wish to change her life's course, but that she felt incapable of turning back. It was irredeemable, so why bother to change? As far as she was concerned, the future was bleak and remained uncertain because it would always be affected by her past. She would say there was no hope. It would never get better – a never-ending cycle of defeat and hopelessness. Laura was locked into this belief system. My hope, however, rested in challenging this thinking and presenting an alternative approach. The hope being that once an alternative was presented, one based on life-changing truths, she would embrace it, thus changing her beliefs, attitudes and values.

Sadly, for Laura this was not to be, as she finds herself pregnant again, in distress again, needing support again. Does this cause me pain? Yes. Am I disappointed? Yes, but fortunately for me, my hope rests in something more. I can continue to speak a message of hope into her life, using my faith, experiences, education and work settings, so that hope is woven throughout the story.

A theology of hope does exist for young people and it is possible to translate it and make connections for young people in whatever role we find ourselves in, often allowing our actions to speak louder than the unspoken word. I will not abandon Laura, for her hope is not yet recovered. Working with her, though, does come with a price – that's the sting in the tail. I must continue, even though it's painful.

A few questions for your own reflection

- How do you cope with the situations that seem hopeless?

- How do you share hope in ways that will not belittle young people's reality and experience, in ways that are authentic and will find resonance with their world?

- What about the notion of ongoing cycles of deprivation and hopelessness?

- Is there a youth work role across generations? If so, what is it, and how do you do it?

Story from the Edge 16:

Dave Horton

Our friend Mark was in a spot of bother. He had got on the wrong side of a gang of lads on the estate and they were out to get him. Apparently this was because he had sold drugs to a gang member's niece, although I never found out whether this was true or not. As a result he was too afraid to leave the house. His school and social life were suffering. Even more worryingly, his mental health was deteriorating. Every day spent under a kind of house arrest made him increasingly depressed and anxious.

We did our best to support him, accompanying him out of the house for trips down to the bay, liaising with the school and making Airfix models with him in his house (something that seemed to help him relax). We also picked him up each week and drove him to the small informal group we ran every Thursday evening on the estate. It was here that Mark asked us to pray that God would protect him from the gang and that he'd soon be able to leave the house safely and without fear. We prayed for him and the rest of the group and dropped him at his door before heading home for a well-earned rest.

At 2:00 the following morning my colleague was woken by a knocking at her front door. It was Mark. He had decided to go camping in a local park with some friends (in hindsight, this was an extraordinary display of faith in the power of our prayers!). At some point in the evening he was located by the gang, dragged from his tent and given a severe kicking. His face and head were bruised and he was pretty shaken up. My colleague spent the rest of the night in the Accident and Emergency ward with him, contacting his parents and sorting out the mess.

I thought about the incident a lot the following day. Apart from being concerned for Mark's well-being after such a vicious incident, I also wondered how he would view our prayers now and how we might make some excuses or put a positive spin on God's oversight! Of course, we never say these things to colleagues or friends; we just find ourselves thinking them sometimes.

The following week was our next group session and Mark was keen to come. We usually liked to discuss with the group whether, and how, prayers had been answered. This week that question seemed to have one obvious answer, and it wasn't the answer we wanted or one that we particularly wanted to confront. Nevertheless, there was no way we could avoid the issue, partly because this would be bad youth work and partly because Mark's still slightly bruised face was a visible reminder of the incident for everyone present. So, eventually, we bit the bullet.

Mark said: "Well, I was out camping with some friends last week, after we prayed that I wouldn't get beaten up. Halfway through the night Liam's gang turned up, dragged me from the tent and started battering me. But then, just when they were really getting stuck in, some lady who was out walking her dog late came running over, shouting at them. As she got closer Liam and his crew ran off. I don't know, but I reckon God answered our prayers and that woman was an angel!"

> *I've never forgotten the faith I saw in one of our slightly lost and broken friends. It is an inspiration and a challenge to my own faithlessness.*

I've thought about Mark's interpretation of those events often since that day. A couple of times Jesus was surprised to find faith in unexpected people and places, and he always made a point of commending that faith and drawing people's attention to it. I've never forgotten the faith I saw in one of our slightly lost and broken friends. It is an inspiration and a challenge to my own faithlessness.

A few questions for your own reflection

- How do you deal with it when the prayers you pray with young people appear not to be answered?

- Do you give space to hear their own interpretations of these situations?

- Are you open to spotting and commending faith in unexpected people and places?

Chapter 4

Youth Culture and Gangs

During my second month of college, our teacher gave us a quiz. I was a conscientious student and had breezed through the questions, until I read the last one: "What is the first name of the woman who cleans the school?" Surely this was some kind of joke. I had seen the cleaning woman several times. She was tall, red and in her 50s, but how would I know her name? I handed in my paper, leaving the last question blank. Just before class ended, one student asked if the last question would count towards our quiz grade. "Absolutely," said the teacher. "In your careers, you will meet many people. All are significant. They deserve your attention and care, even if all you do is smile and say 'hello.'" I've never forgotten that lesson. I also learned her name was Dorothy.

Source unknown

"Guys – do you mind being a bit quieter? My daughter is trying to get to sleep, and it's eleven o'clock at night!"

This, I thought, was a reasonable request of the youngsters gathered outside our house for their weekly session of Triple X and cannabis.

"Why don't you go and sing her a ****ing lullaby!" replied the lad sitting on our garden wall. I had just left my nine-year-old daughter in tears because she couldn't sleep, so this was the wrong reply for me just at that moment!

My mind spun back to my own adolescence: drugs, fights, image creation and turbulent hormones. I wish I could say that I had returned to these insights to reflect upon and understand the perspective of my aggressive friend. However, it was more a consideration of whether or not I dared to decorate my garden with his face!

Thankfully, I managed to control my own temper. Again I tried to appeal to the more humane side of his persona – I guessed it was buried somewhere amidst the chemicals. I could at least appeal to an existing relationship with him and his friends. I often stopped to talk with them, whether or not they were sober. Eventually they tired of baiting me and peace was restored.

In actual fact, over the next few weeks things got a bit better. I wondered if my drip-feed relationship building was working. Several weeks later I went out to the group with a small reward for the improved behaviour.

"I know you would prefer fags," I said, "but I thought these would be slightly better for you." I handed a large bag of toffees to the gang leader, saying, "Thanks for being so quiet recently."

I wished I had a camera! To see a group of seventeen-year-olds sat on their motorbikes, barely concealing a pleasure that they were not sure they wanted to express, was a wonderful experience for me.

"Cheers, mate," was the stammered reply.

I walked into my home realizing how different things might have been, had my own temper got the better of me a few weeks ago.

I was also left thinking about how our perspectives of young people so often determine the way they act towards us. I remembered a friend who worked in an inner-city parish with local youngsters returning to the church where her husband was the vicar. They had been to the chip shop on a cold winter's night and were looking for somewhere to eat

I was also left thinking about how our perspectives of young people so often determine the way they act towards us.

as they sheltered from the rain. My friend let them into the church and they gravitated to the only table they could find – the one at the front with the colourful tablecloth decorated with grapes and bread!

As they shared their chips around the altar, in the hushed sombre atmosphere of the dying day, my friend realized that the feelings she was experiencing were those she normally associated with taking communion. These moments spent in fellowship around the table were taking on a sacramental meaning. That is, until the churchwarden barged in with a differing perspective! He saw the feast as sacrilegious and asked them to leave. I wonder what the young people thought of these differing perspectives.

There is much speculation and opinion about youth culture and gangs and how best to work amongst them. I have met Christians who see the potential for working with gangs as a kind of glamorous voyeurism that they seem almost euphoric about in an unhealthy way. On the other hand, I have come across youth workers who have "gone native" and all but assimilated the values and behaviours of the young people they are with. How do we understand youth culture and gangs, and how can we work within the differing contexts that young people grow up in?

A need to belong

I was a serial group participant when I was growing up. I am sure that the rejection and lack of attachment that I experienced in my early years ensured that I was desperate for the affirmation and acceptance of my friends. I need to be needed, I want to be wanted and I love to be loved, and I suspect this is central to the human condition.

The debate about peer influence in adolescence is important. I would argue that it is not a phenomenon that is unique to children and young people. Adults are just as fixated with their need to belong as are young people. The need to be with others who are similar to you or of a like mind, is a basic human need that is quite normal. (For example, see Maslow's hierarchy of need, which outlines our physiological needs as well as those needs that are about safety, love, belonging, esteem and self-actualization.)

Do groups of young people with pink Mohican haircuts, safety-pinned lips and Sex Pistol T-shirts look that much more threatening than blue-rinsed elderly ladies in twin sets and pearls who frown at anyone under fifty? Groups of Christians that convene around particular traditions and theologies can seem just as blinkered and narrow as young people who coalesce around forms of music or activities like skating or free running.

I moved from group to group in rapid succession as a young person.

I wore Levi jeans, Doc Marten boots and granddad T-shirts in my skinhead phase; I spent a while wearing Oxford Bag Trousers and Ben Sherman shirts as part of the suedehead youth culture; I stopped washing my jeans and called them 'originals' when I signed up for the "Devil's Disciples" biker gang; and I wore flowers as a hippie.

Of course, the "uniform" is only one aspect of association and conformity in youth culture. The affiliation to certain types of music – like reggae for skinheads (who are, ironically, often very racist), heavy rock for greasers (Hells Angels etc.), and psychedelic for hippies – offers clues to the chosen group identity of the individual.

Patterns of behaviour are also adopted to confirm "membership" of a certain group. Despite my own deep-down misgivings, I found myself engaged in racist and fascist violence as a skinhead; I got wasted on alcohol when driving motorbikes as a "Devil's Disciple"; and I took all the mandatory, non-prescribed drugs as a hippie.

Scorn at the behaviour of young people is nothing new. Apparently the Greek philosopher Plato complained about the youth of his day, saying:

> *What is happening to our young people? They disrespect their elders, they disobey their parents. They ignore the law. They riot in the streets, inflamed with wild notions. Their morals are decaying. What is to become of them?*

Questions about the existence and influence of youth culture abound. The reaction of the law, the media and wider society to youth cultures is fascinating and is often proved by sociologists and psychologists to be far from neutral and value-free acceptance of the "need to belong".

Gang membership

Gang membership is a fascinating phenomenon.

It was a cold night and I hugged my Prince of Wales checked Crombie tightly as we looked for the next bunch of innocents to harass. It didn't matter who we "had it out" with – tramps were a favourite target, or those who frequented gay bars, or those with a skin colour different to our own. We were just looking for "bovver". It eventually came in the shape of a pub brawl, where glasses were the only weapons. Pick-axe handles were reserved for out-of-town sorties. Thank God we didn't have access to guns so easily in the sixties!

My own brief involvement in gangs during the late sixties and early seventies leaves me ashamed and often leads to sober reflection upon the grace of God. I confess that the experience has stood me in good stead in terms of street credibility in my youth work. I seem to have a natural connecting point with the youngsters on the estates where I have worked.

My exploits from the past often have become urban myth and young people recognize the empathy I seem to have with them. Encounters with adults who feel that we should just "hang or flog" gang members (or drug pushers, for that matter) often end with embarrassing silences when I mention my own past as both a gang member and a drug pusher. The world is never as simple as we might hope; it's certainly not as simple as the populist press would have us think.

> The world is never as simple as we might hope; it's certainly not as simple as the populist press would have us think.

I have unqualified sympathy for those who are the victims of gang activity and would argue strongly for greater provision of victim support services. But I would also want to suggest that the kind of fascist attitudes that some opinion formers propagate about young people who are involved in gangs is a disservice to understanding, or any hope of progress and change for those young people. A more balanced position is argued by Steve Beebee of the National Youth Agency, who points out that:

> *Although the rise [of gangs] cannot be reasonably compared to the impression given by certain sections of the media, and while the use of firearms remains relatively rare, there is no doubt that gangs pose an increasing threat to young people, especially those living in inner city areas.*[8]

His report goes on to outline some of the key problems relating to gangs and offers some youth work responses in terms of case studies. It also provides some helpful action points relating to youth work principles. Tom Wylie (then

Chief Executive of NYA) concludes the report by suggesting that whilst wanting to support the government's agenda in responding to antisocial behaviour, we need to prove the value of youth work's contribution in responding to young people in gangs. The report ends by stating that the key thing is for youth workers to stand by the young people that we work with, even though we may only be able to make small changes, and that we should build and sustain work arising from community reaction to local events. This, of course, has to be the million-dollar question – how do you respond to this kind of issue in communities that will obviously be threatened, angry and even grieving, in the face of gang activity, especially violence?

I have carried out research[9] amongst Christian youth workers, and this offers some clues about the issues that young people face in gangs and how we might respond to them. The research is tentative, as it was based on a limited sample of youth workers who were directly involved in work with gangs and others who were aware of youth work by Christians in this arena.

Issues faced by young people in gangs

In his book *God and the Gangs*, Robert Beckford articulates so well the tension between the individual responsibility of gang members in relation to their behaviours and the social or structural context in which such behaviour takes place, as well as the way in which black young people are particularly vulnerable:

> *There is no justifiable reason for condoning drug dealing and the use of weapons. However, it remains essential that we address the systematic failure which shows itself in structural breakdown within families, law, education and employment. Gun crime and gang violence is made in urban Britain... Many of the black youths involved in gun crime were born and raised during the Conservative reign of the 1980s... warehoused in substandard schools, ignored in under-funded communities and sent to young offenders' institutions and prisons in disproportionate numbers. We are reaping a grim harvest from the brutal assault on urban social amenities, family structures and employment possibilities...[10]*

This sentiment is reflected in my own study. Many of the participants did not want to separate young people in gangs from other marginalized young people. Respondents offered insights into the need to address an unfair society as well as insights into the behaviour of those involved in gangs. The specific themes and issues that were mentioned by those involved in my research as being significant social factors included:

Employment

Responses ranged from explanations that seemed social in nature – "poor employment opportunities" through to explanations that seemed more focused on personal responsibility – "they enjoy hanging around and 'working' with each other". It was claimed that "They don't like being told what to do" and doing menial jobs, which makes them unsuitable for work. In addition, the suggestion is that gang activities may have yielded a criminal conviction, making constructive activity even more difficult.

Employment has to be an important issue and I would want to endorse the work of national projects, like Worth Unlimited, that enable young people to explore their own sense of identity and self-worth, as well as helping with securing employment. The current rise in unemployment figures, which are attributed to recession, is a worrying phenomenon for young people and those of us who work with them.

Educational achievement

This issue is linked to employment. It was noted that it was not necessarily applicable to all gang members; however, it is a common occurrence. The educational system that we have developed is not effective for so many young people and projects that provide "tailored" education are critical. Projects and schemes which help young people to cope with their current educational experiences are also crucial – for example, the small group work programmes (such as RAMP, Re-engaging And Motivating Pupils) run by local authorities and others around the UK. These offer programmes to enable young people to explore their own behaviour, anger management, social skills and a whole host of themes that enable them to cope with their educational and home environment. Tragically, these efforts are all too often under-funded, over-dependent on temporary funding or closed down, as they are not valued enough.

Sexual health and drug use/misuse

This was a frequently mentioned issue that young people in gangs face. A number of the projects that participants were involved in were offering guidance, advice and information. I have been particularly encouraged at the number of Christian projects that have moved beyond narrow moralistic debates about the provision of information and services in this area, and are seeking to reduce harm rather than purely promote abstinence.

Identity and peer pressure

These were cited by participants as being of particular concern. Gang membership itself can be seen as evidence that identity and peer pressure are even more pertinent for the young people involved in gangs than other young people. This kind of psychological dynamic is illuminated by one respondent who said, "They become intolerant to how other people live, they can't cope with weakness because as a unit they will always be strong and they will never see themselves as worth anything because their worth is in the gang."

Gun crimes and violence

This was predictably mentioned by a number of respondents, not only in terms of the fear and concern that this creates in wider society but in terms of the fear it generates between gangs and amongst young people. For example, one person said, "There is a fear of other gangs; this becomes a fear of moving off the estates for fear of being shot. Inter- and intra-gang rivalry can mean they get shot. Death is a big issue."

Responding to young people in gangs

Youth workers have the ability to meet young people where they are, emotionally and socially, through a number of methodologies, and some workers are committed to building relationships over a long period of time. Many youth workers do not represent statutory bodies, and although they need to be aware of legal issues, they can be perceived as a less threatening form of authority in the lives and experience of young people in gangs. Youth workers are often able to discuss issues with young people in a more relaxed and candid manner. Current practice and ideas shared by participants in my research suggest that the following roles, that youth workers might adopt, may be of significance in working with young people in gangs:

Diversionary activities

This means engaging in activities that are legitimate and respond to the young person's need to "let off steam". One worker wrote that youth work should "open up avenues of legitimate activity. Help them understand the harm they cause and the impact on others. Tackle underlying issues, which prevent them from moving forward and realizing their potential."

Alan Duncan (a Conservative MP) spent a week, courtesy of a reality TV programme (*My Week in the Real World*), as a youth worker in Manchester. During this time he took a group of local youngsters, who exhibited some seriously "challenging behaviours", to a residential "outdoor experience" in North Wales. It was a fascinating programme for many reasons, but perhaps mostly because of the way a senior politician was so easily won over to the value of youth work (and particularly diversionary youth work) in so short a period. He ended the week vowing never to demean youth workers as wishy-washy liberals! I wish that governments were as quick to invest in diversionary work.

Preventative and educational work

Working with those young people who are thinking about gang membership. This kind of work is raising awareness about the associated risks and dangers and seeking to reduce harm. One worker wrote: "I have contact with some younger guys on the edge of some gangs in the area where I work and can provide an informative and educative role with those on the fringe of gang involvement." As one worker put it, youth workers can offer support as a mentor, a significant adult, and a more objective sounding-board to discuss consequences and options.

Of course, this does raise concerns about safety, risk and a number of procedural questions about how workers engage with gangs. However, it is important to note the potential that this kind of relationship has in informing, educating and supporting young people in gangs. The value of detached street work projects around the country should not be underestimated in their contribution to this kind of activity.

Relationship formation

The importance of forming non-judgmental relationships with young people in gangs was identified as critical. One respondent said that things like friendship, acceptance and love could redress the balance of life and create a better purpose in life for gang members. Whilst not wanting to understate the grief and pain that gangs can cause to others, many of the workers wanted to emphasize the damaged sense of self-worth that gang members can have about themselves. They underlined the importance of responding to the gang members' need for an inner sense of worth and value.

It is important not to underestimate the power of providing a "listening ear and a safe place to be", as one worker expressed it. To young people who may have had traumatic relationships with adults as they have grown up, and who now face the seemingly endless barrage of hostile adults who seek to control their behaviour, a trusting relationship with a youth worker might be a real point of development and positive change.

Mediation

The importance of mediation in the youth worker role was recognized, particularly as gangs can be misunderstood and are subjected to a number of stereotypical attitudes. A youth worker may be well placed to enable understanding between differing groups in a community or in wider society. Mediation may occur between adults and young people, professionals and community groups, or indeed between differing groups/gangs of young people. As one worker put it, "A youth worker can act as a mediator to help bring opposing gangs together to share common stories. By building relationships with both parties there may be opportunities to discuss openly how gang culture affects those involved."

I would like to challenge those of us engaged in Christian youth ministry to rethink our calling to young people in gangs as well as those who are on the other edges of our society. I want to argue for action which responds to causes (what some, like Robert Beckford, would call "prophetic action") as well as symptoms in relation to the issues raised by gang activity. After all, Jesus didn't call us to be peace-lovers, but peace-makers.

Some further thinking, reflection and stories

The Joseph Rowntree Trust has done some extremely helpful research[11] into young people in gangs within four neighbourhoods of Glasgow amongst 231 parents and 259 young people. A summary of their findings is well worth consideration:

- Despite high levels of low income, unemployment and drug misuse, both parents and young people usually identified positive aspects in their local areas, particularly associated with the presence of familiar and trusted family, friends and neighbours.

- Parents and children reported coping with a wide range of local risks to the children's immediate and long-term well-being. Their main concerns centred on threats from youth gangs and from adults or young people misusing drugs and alcohol.

- Parents believed that promoting organized, supervised activities reduced the likelihood of their children coming into contact with risks, provided safe alternatives and offered opportunities for skill development and social development.

- Parents described parenting styles that were open, democratic, sophisticated and tenacious in working alongside their children to keep them safe. This challenges views that parenting problems are rife in areas with high levels of antisocial behaviour by young people.

- Children usually valued parents' interest and rules as showing concern for them although, particularly as they got older, they would sometimes ignore or subvert parental rules to create their own space and independence.

- Young people took responsibility for keeping themselves and their friends safe by sharing knowledge, looking out for each other and moving around together. They used their detailed local knowledge to avoid or minimize hazardous situations. Some were aware that certain adults saw such self-protective groups as threatening.

- Parents often had high aspirations for their children, based on realistic assessments of their children's strengths. However, the capacity to fulfil such hopes, especially educational ones, relied on knowledge and resources that many parents may lack.

- In protecting their children from the effects of low income, parents showed a high degree of creativity and budgetary skill. Parents were very conscious of peer and commercial pressures to buy desired items and clothes that were hard to afford.

The research points to a number of specific implications across a range of policy areas. These include:

- Developing policies which are consistent with the many strengths and aspirations of parents and young people living in disadvantaged areas, as well as seeking to tackle some of the risk factors, including gang activity and drug/alcohol misuse.

- Ensuring that national and local policies work with and promote informal networks that share information about safe activities and provide practical advice and support. Such networks are at the core of parents' strategies to keep young people safe in high-risk communities. The time it takes for these networks to develop should not be underestimated.

- Integrating socially isolated parents, as isolation from these networks can compound the experience of social exclusion and the difficult nature of parenting in high-risk situations.

- Challenging over-simple assumptions that areas have a negative culture of parenting and that peer-group activity is largely antisocial.

- Schools capitalizing on the evidence of parents' commitment to discussion and discipline, with parents acting as allies in behaviour management for school staff, even in challenging areas.

- Provision of a range of low-cost leisure facilities in disadvantaged communities, which maximize inclusion and safety at all times, to enhance children's social and educational resilience.

A few questions for your own reflection

- How do you see youth cultures and gangs?

- What has shaped and informed your opinions and how do these impact your attitudes and behaviours?

- How else might you understand this phenomenon?

- What are good strategies for working with young people in differing youth cultures and gangs?

- How do you engage meaningfully, safely and constructively?

- What models do you know of that work, and why do they seem to work?

Story from the Edge 17:

Peter Hope

It would be fair to say that village life in winter for young people is a dull, drab affair. The Youth Service pulled out of my village some time ago, closing the youth centre, leaving a small contingent of youngsters to their own devices and a rural community at odds as to how to respond.

Antisocial behaviour and "yob culture" are major media and political themes at the moment. Vandalism, rowdiness, drugs, alcohol – you could be forgiven for thinking that every youngster was engaged in such activities. Some obviously are, and the reasons may be complex, but perhaps it might be because there are few alternatives that catch their imagination or can provide a buzz. Young people in villages are no different from young people in towns or cities. Boredom and isolation seem to me to be big factors in antisocial behaviour.

As a church we responded, establishing relationships with the youngsters who had been evicted from their youth centre to make way for housing. We integrated them into an existing youth club running from the church. We provide space for them to chill out, sporting activities, music, dance, residential experiences and trips to engage with them. Plans have even progressed for an internet café, and a motorbike club. We had to cap our numbers at fifty, with an active membership of around seventy-five. There are about 250 secondary-school-age young people in the village.

It has not been easy, and not without cost or friction. There is a group of a dozen fifteen–sixteen year-olds who frequent the club. Anywhere else

they would be described as a gang. They do everything together and wear the same "chav" (Council House And Violent) uniform. They are inseparable. Several have been excluded from school and are in trouble with the police. They try to live up to their reputation as being "untouchable". They are derided by some of their peers, many of whom feel intimidated by them.

There is an established group of young lads in the club who we have worked with for several years. Initially they were a handful! We encouraged them to play for a football team, which I manage, and they have become firm friends as a result. They come from similar backgrounds as the group of "chavs". The two groups detest each other with a passion. Club nights are interesting evenings! The "chavs" look upon the footballers as rivals.

Having worked with young people in the village for well over a decade, it's hard to be anonymous. People know where I live, what I drink in the pub, what motorbike I ride, what football team I support. I know what it's like to be a goldfish in a bowl!

The reality of that was fully emphasized one evening when one of the footballers knocked on my door. He was dishevelled and shaken, bruised and frightened. A group of the "chavs" had assaulted him and stolen his mobile phone, wallet and keys. He couldn't get into his house to ring his parents, who were away. We calmed him down; my wife fed him and comforted him.

The following night was club night. The lad knew who his assailants were, and so did I. That evening I challenged them over the incident, and barred five of them. I fully expected the rest of the "chavs" to follow their mates, and I thought there would also be some reprisals against the building. But instead, there was a protracted conversation amongst the group. I had explained that the ban would be lifted if there were no further incidents and the property was returned to the victim, but for that evening I was not allowing them into the club. I also told them the matter was in the hands of the police.

The five who were involved slunk off, with no denials, with one other lad who they had pressurized to go with them, but six others decided to stay. The six had done nothing wrong, and encouraged me by saying that the club was all they had. They enjoyed the sessions and they wanted to come in. They came in and, for the first time, were able to integrate with the whole of the group. We had a good session.

The following day the lad who had been assaulted came round to thank us for the support. He also expressed his surprise that his phone, wallet and keys had been returned – he had found them on his front lawn that morning. But more surprisingly, one of the offending group had apologized to him that day.

Life in the village and the club rolls on. The ban was lifted on the five, who came back. The lad who was attacked was able to come, confident in the knowledge that he was in a safe place. A few glares were exchanged, some of the "chavs" nodded at him, a couple spoke to him, and then we got on with a game of dodge-ball. I don't suppose this will be last incident with this group. They have no part-time jobs, no transport and they have family and social problems. For a few, we are all they have, but we only provide one evening a week. They're worth a lot more than that, and so is peace in our communities.

A few questions for your own reflection

- What kinds of groups/gangs exist in your area? How do you relate to them and between them?

- What are the essential skills of being a peace-maker in youth work?

- How long do you need to work in a community to get to know how best to respond to inter-group rivalry?

- What has youth work got to offer to groups/gangs and how do we relate to them effectively?

Story from the Edge 18:
A Frontier Youth Trust networker [anonymous]

In our youth club the rules, as in most places, included no smoking, drinking or doing drugs on the premises; our rules also applied to the car park. It was large and had security staff at times, but on club nights no one would be around except the volunteer staff members and the youths, most of whom lived locally and walked in.

As with many clubs, we had a core membership and then others who would come in now and again. Some, often those perceived as the "toughest" ones, wouldn't actually come into the building but would hover at the edge of the car park, and because of our hard line on smoking there was also a corner where the smokers would gather, just off the main road. Sometimes staff members would be based there, working with those who were hanging around outside.

On several occasions a couple of cars full of young people would drive in and the guys would just sit listening to music. They wouldn't want to come in except for the occasional cuppa, but nor did they want to go. Although the car park was private, once we'd asked the young people to join in the club or leave (which they didn't), there was little we could do, unless they did anything really bad (which they didn't). We didn't want to get the police in and alienate them further, but the cars were a real draw for younger girls from the club, particularly because they were often full of older lads.

It's difficult being a church-based open youth club worker, because you always have to hold in tension the views of church members, the youth team, parents and the local community, not to mention the youths themselves. In one sense there was no issue here, and you could say we were being paranoid, but any mention of out-of-order behaviour in our car park, and I'm sure that some church members would be questioning the abilities of the youth club's staff.

It was very difficult to stop the girls going out to the cars, but at fourteen, they were not young children. So we were left with a dilemma, really. Once they were in the cars it was impossible to control their behaviour, such as who was "getting off" with whom. And there were rumours of bottles of spirits, colourful reputations and drugs. The sometimes naïve young girls might leave with a bunch of older guys who'd been drinking and driving, and then what about safety? What if they did not arrive back before the end of club, and then whose responsibility were they?

We couldn't lock people into the club, and some parents wouldn't have known that their kids were even at the club anyway. They certainly wouldn't expect us to force them to stay away from anyone else; but then, in many other people's eyes, the youth workers were *in loco parentis* once the young people were at the club. Some of the church parents would have thought us very irresponsible for not "protecting" their young people. Perhaps, also, they would blame us when "interesting" relationships were formed which might lead their kids off the straight and narrow.

For us, every occasion had to be dealt with as an individual case. We tended to think of young people as our responsibility once they had signed in and seen a copy of the club rules. If they were leaving the club activities, we would try to get them to sign out too. Obviously we'd always try to encourage new people inside, which stopped them being "demonized" as the ones who'd be blamed for any trouble. And, of course, it was essential to make the club a great place once they were inside.

Without security on the car-park entrance, you can't stop people driving in. It's also very difficult to force people to leave who don't want to go, so what would you have done?

A few questions for your own reflection

- Do you have enough staff to post people outside as well as inside?

- Are you aware of how far your legal obligations to young people go?

- You can't search a person or a car outside a youth club, but how do you minimize the potential risk of drugs being brought in?

- How do you use physical space in your youth work and how does it affect your relationships?

Story from the Edge 19:

Matt Robinson

"I hate this. I want to go back to the centre. There's no bog..."

Ten teenagers all complaining at once, using some fairly strong language, as they had been for the past half hour. Actually, some had been complaining for the past few days:

"I'm not staying here – it's filthy."

"I don't want tea – it looks horrible."

"We all have to sleep on the floor – in the same room!"

"Matt says the loo is that spade – uurgh!"

"My spare clothes are wet – and my new kit is covered in mud."

And so on...!

The walk had taken us most of the day – getting up over the wide, high-level ridge and then turning right and descending the steep valley to our night's accommodation. We had started off in hot conditions, scrambling up through the deep bracken, then through the really steep rocks. The view was non-existent, and some people were tired, having not had much sleep the previous few nights, and were sulking or arguing with each other. As we got to the top of the first peak, one of the lads was out in front, showing us all the way. At least he was having a good time.

From there on the weather got worse, until we finally had to resort to some careful work with the compass and regular head-counts in the mist. I had to agree that the last part of the ridge was grotty, wet and cold. Poor Jackie then fell in the bog on the last leg down the valley to the bothy.

The bothy was basic by some standards, luxurious by others. It had an upstairs sleeping area, a wood-burning stove and a kitchen. Someone had dragged up a few chairs and tables, and there was always the visitors' book to read and laugh at. Upon arrival, the group raced round, excited to be there, exploring everything.

Soon the complaining started. One of them asked for the loo. I don't think the answer, "See the trees over there? Well, take the spade and go into the edge of the wood" was the answer she wanted! Neither were "We all sleep upstairs together" and "You all have to cook your own food, and don't forget to wash up."

We waded through tea, got the fire going and started to clear up after ourselves. The arguments continued. Some of the group were turning on each other.

I sat in the doorway, looking out into the gloom of the early evening mist. Why were we here? Most of these kids saw the hills as a nice view as they walked down Sauchiehall Street, and they didn't even get to see them today. We were miles from the minibus, and they weren't up to walking out tonight. They were tired, ill at ease, probably scared and definitely did not want to be there. They had come for a holiday – someone had raised the money for them to come – not to be miserable. What were we thinking of? "Oh, you'll enjoy it!"

How do I witness about Jesus' love when they won't speak to me? Why do we take youngsters from the place where they feel comfortable?

How do you befriend someone who resents you bringing them out to this foreign place that they hate? How do I witness about Jesus' love when they won't speak to me? Would they go away with a view of God's kingdom being a smelly bothy? Why do we take youngsters from the place where they feel comfortable? Many people use the day out, the residential or outdoor experience, to help in their outreach, but do we really understand why we use this tool?

By eleven o'clock the group had calmed down. Some of them had helped light the fire, others had made hot chocolate for everyone, and someone put a load of candles out to light up the pitch-black room. Mind you, they had too much energy to go to sleep and had started to get wound up, chasing each other round, up and down the ladder, and throwing things. I glanced outside and it was bone dry; the full moon was out.

"Let's go for a walk!" I said, to a chorus of "You must be joking!" "Get off!"

"No, we're going out," I insisted.

As we set out for the walk, the group fell into a line. A few were quite nervous. We turned the torches off and could see really well. We started to chat and joke and laugh about the day. Tom had fallen out of the canoe and Kylie had gone down the zip-wire screaming her head off! "And do you remember...?" and so on. We got back at one or two in the morning (I didn't notice). We had spent ages throwing rocks into the loch. I had taught them how to "skim", using sticks as targets. We'd spent a lot of time shouting, yelling and playing hide and seek. We'd talked about their lives and our own. The other instructors agreed, it was the highlight of the week.

The following day, we walked back to the bus, face on into a gale and heavy rain. No one complained, we were all larking around, chatting and sharing sweets around. We got back exhausted to the centre, had a shower and gathered round the fire to warm up and laugh at the other group who had set off this morning to go and stay in a bothy.

A few questions for your own reflection

- Do we really understand some of the youth work tools and contexts that we use?

- Was I in control of the situation? I did nothing different, yet the breakthrough in relationship on that midnight walk was total.

- Does relating to a child or young person on the street, meeting them "where they are at", make any difference? Does territory, environment and context make much difference?

- What difference does working in the outdoors make, if any?

- Was this night out alienating or a shared, common experience?

- How can we create a shared, common experience on "neutral" territory without having to go on such an extreme trip?

This poem, written by a young person, is a powerful reminder of the importance of place in youth work:

> *When I'm here*
> *I feel at peace*
> *Nobody to annoy me*
> *My tension is released.*
>
> *I never feel lonely*
> *Or ever left out*
> *Everyone is friendly*
> *And mucking about.*
>
> *Anyone can stay here*
> *And feel the same as I*
> *You forget about your problems*
> *Above them you will fly.*

Story from the Edge 20:
Matt and Diane Hall

"Oi, what are you lot doing up that tree?!" was met with no response other than a collective nervous giggle. Eventually the half dozen teenage boys clambered down from the tree and slunk off out of our garden in Easterhouse, Glasgow. They were unable to explain why they hadn't knocked on the door and merely asked if they could play in the garden.

This may seem a wee bit extreme – our response, that is, not the young people's – but I hope this story may open up a discussion of issues such as a respect for personal space, boundaries and seeking permission.

After living in the estate for just under a year, we moved into a ground-floor flat with a large corner garden. As we had begun by sharing our home with local young people, we felt that this new abode with a garden was an extension of that. We took this position to give the young people a safe and peaceful space in which to play and enjoy creation. Through this we hoped to communicate that we wanted to share what God had given us.

This sharing of the garden is based upon a few conditions. Young people must ask first if they want to use the garden. Their parents must know us and must know that their child is visiting us. Sometimes we say no, because we need a break from the work; or because it's too late in the day, and so children playing in the garden might annoy our neighbours; or because we are not at home to say yes. This last condition is mainly a safety issue. For example, what if someone falls off a tree when we're not in? It is also about teaching respect for others' personal space and the boundaries that have been set. However, because of the thrill of doing something they know they shouldn't be doing, "no" is often taken to mean "yes"! We often return to find the swing hanging down from the tree, a sure sign that someone has been playing while we've been away. Is the hanging swing a symbol of defiance, or is it because the culprits are not clever enough to hide the evidence?

I would say that most of the time, young people are allowed to play in the garden and they respect the boundaries. If they get a little too familiar or cheeky, they respond well to being asked to leave. If we do have to ask them to leave, they know that the ban will only be for a short period, unless there is ongoing disrespect.

We do hope that the garden is a place of belonging and a space to build relationships and enjoy creation. Some of the best chats we have had with young people have been when we've been gardening or sitting out on the odd sunny Glasgow day. We also don't have to turn away young people if only one of us is in. (For child protection reasons, both of us have to be in for a young person to come into the house.)

Another low-key, natural context to build relationships is when we have one of our increasingly famous barbecues – even if we get half of the estate's dope smokers who are feeling the "munchies". This is an opportunity to chat with people we've been praying for. They've come to us – we've not forced ourselves upon them for an uncomfortable, monosyllabic conversation!

But there is a challenge when you share your personal space, especially one which you can't put a lock on (and you don't necessarily want to). Many of the issues raised here need to be worked out beforehand if you are a youth worker living on the patch. Obviously, there are ongoing challenges. But ongoing grace is what enables you to persevere.

A few questions for your own reflection

- When you are living on the patch, what boundaries do you think are important for your personal space? [You need to think of time out and space for you and your family.]

- Do you find it difficult to be consistent with these boundaries?

- Have you thought of involving young people you work with in making agreed boundaries for your personal space?

- What have you set in place to ensure the care and protection of young people when they are using your personal space [e.g. house, garden, car, a room in a public space]?

Story from the Edge 21:

Peter Hope

"Naaaaaaah! Basket-ball hoops in a church?! Blimey, what's going on here, then?"

I had expected a negative reaction from some of the church members, and approval from the youngsters, who had asked for a basket-ball amenity, but I was a little taken aback by Mal's shocked expression.

My relationship with Mal began over five years ago. He came from a split home, with a father, two stepfathers, half a dozen stepbrothers and stepsisters, plus his own bloodline siblings. Events had moved quickly in his life. He had been farmed out to various relatives as he reacted to the strains of the new relationships around him, but now he had returned.

He has some notoriety in the local community. He spray-paints and leaves his "tag" all over the place. Mostly, everyone knows it's him, but he thinks he is "un-sussed".

He also got driven over and had his leg broken in two places while playing "chicken" with the local traffic! The repaired leg was further broken on a bicycle stunt that went wrong.

He still came to the club I ran, and insisted on playing badminton in plaster and on crutches. I explained the liability issue, the risk assessment, my responsibilities and so on, but he told me to go forth and multiply, confidently informing me that he could beat anyone hopping on one leg. I said "fair enough" and asked the other players if they were happy to play. They were highly amused and wanted him there for the entertainment value.

At the first passage of play he ended up in a heap on the floor, having missed his shot whilst lifting his crutch. Gales of laughter, then an embarrassed Mal hopped off the court, admitting defeat. He is a character, who has seen much during his fifteen years. I have to admit he is a handful, but I like him.

Mal belongs to a gang who think they are "untouchable", but the local constabulary have caught up with them! And in reality, they have excluded themselves from the local community, who have tried to work with them.

Our club is the only place they go to. They can chill out, play football, pool, badminton, table-tennis, Playstation, air-hockey – all the normal paraphernalia, except that all this is in a church. Even for Mal, allowing basket-ball hoops actually in the church was something shocking, not because he disagreed – he loved the idea – it was just that the hoops were permanent, not temporary things that got put away like everything else. It was a symbol of acceptance to him, far beyond the Scripture readings or testimonies we have tried in the past.

The basket-ball sessions we now run are a regular feature of the club. A local coach comes in and the lads have to play by the rules. It's umpired strictly, but fairly. Masking-tape boundaries mark the court, and a plastic-coated sponge-ball replaces the heavier basket-ball. The lads love it. This is all going on beneath a cross marked with the words, "For anyone who believes in the Lord Jesus Christ will be saved."

As Mal left the club on the first night he played basket-ball, he offered me a high five. "Respect!" was his parting word as our palms clashed.

It's taken ten years of graft in this church to get to this point, leaving me to reflect that respect is hard won but well worth the effort.

A few questions for your own reflection

- This story raises questions about the use of church buildings, and indeed the meaning of "church" in youth work.

- What issues have you faced? How is youth work seen by your church contacts and young people?

- What is your view about the spiritual and social interface of your youth work practice?

- How should we relate to gangs?

Chapter 5

On the Road: Interpersonal Contemplation

There once was a little boy who wanted to meet God. He knew it was a long trip to where God lived, so he packed his suitcase with Penguin bars and some cans of Coke, and he started his journey.

When he had travelled about a quarter of a mile, he met an old man. He was sitting in the park, just staring at some pigeons. The boy sat down next to him and opened his suitcase. He was about to take a drink of Coke when he noticed that the old man looked hungry, so he offered him a Penguin.

He gratefully accepted it and smiled at him. His smile was so incredible that the boy wanted to see it again, so he offered him a Coke. Once again, the old man smiled at him.

The boy was delighted! They sat there all afternoon eating, drinking and smiling, but they never said a word. As it grew dark, the boy realized how tired he was and he got up to leave, but before he had gone more than a few steps, he turned around, ran back to the old man, and gave him a hug. The old man gave him his biggest smile ever.

When the boy opened the door to his own house a short time later, his mother was surprised by the look of joy on his face. She asked him, "What did you do today that made you so happy?"

He replied, "I had lunch with God." But before his mother could respond, he added, "You know what? He's got the most beautiful smile I've ever seen!"

Meanwhile, the old man, also radiant with joy, returned to his home. His son was stunned by the look of peace on his face and he asked, "Dad, what did you do today that made you so happy?"

He replied, "I ate Penguins in the park with God." But before his son responded, he added, "You know, he's much younger than I expected."

Source unknown

This chapter recounts an "adventure" in what I call "interpersonal contemplation" that Tim Evans and I had when we spent a week on the road together. With only £10 in our pockets – with no plans, no hotels, no transport and, some would say, no sense – our journey began! We did this in order to launch an initiative in which young people used ten pounds as a way to raise funding for a youth-led trust fund. We also wanted to generate positive stories about young people, and we did this by asking those we met on the road to share stories of hope with us. This chapter was largely written by Tim and I jointly, so collective nouns will tend to be used throughout.

For five days we travelled between Bristol, Cardiff, Birmingham and Liverpool, with no resources or arrangements other than contact with local youth work projects and radio stations. We saw this as an alternative model for Christian leaders to promote their ideas – a substitute for large-scale Christian PR campaigns! We came back from our journey with £4 in our pockets, having given away £5 and spent £1 on chocolate, and we give thanks to God and his people for the care, generosity and love that we received. The journey was a reminder that faith is spelt "R-I-S-K", and we received so much more than we gave through our pilgrimage together. But now – back to the beginning...

Group encounters

We started by walking away from the railway station, praying that God would be in our journey and that we would be able to make a small contribution to challenging what we perceived to be a "dominant narrative" about young people that is rooted in suspicion, fear, generalizations and stereotypes. Neither of us is naïve about young people's potential to behave "badly". However, bad behaviour is not the full story and we wanted to make a contribution to sharing something about the more positive side of young people, by listening to their stories and sharing them with a wider audience. We very nearly missed our first opportunity to listen to young people as we passed a large group enjoying their cigarette break. However, we crossed the road.

> *Bad behaviour is not the full story and we wanted to make a contribution to sharing something about the more positive side of young people.*

The group we spoke with were cautious to begin with – two middle-aged guys approaching them out of the blue! However, the initial caution turned into very real supportive interest in our journey. We chatted about their training and discovered that we had stumbled upon a Youth Training Scheme. Here were a group of young people engaging in the government's agenda for education and employment. They were warm, welcoming and communicative, despite the fact that some of them may have been labelled as "Not in Education, Employment or Training" (NEET) by government definitions.

Their thoughts about hope were interesting and each of them spoke about the way they and their friends looked after each other, especially when alcohol was involved. On the one hand, it is important to express concern about binge drinking and the associated short- and long-term risks it presents to young people; and on the other hand, it is also important to remember that this is not the whole story. These young people had all been involved with supporting and looking after their friends when they had used too much alcohol. They had patted the backs of their friends whilst they had vomited in toilets and sinks, and they had even cleaned up when the target was missed!

After about fifteen minutes of conversation we left the young people, who wished us well on our journey and waved us goodbye. It occurred to us that these youngsters may well have been seen as a gang of threatening youths by us and others at times, yet here they were, providing us with a positive, respectful and sincere response.

We had the notion of going to St Paul's, a district of Bristol with a notorious reputation, according to some, after the so-called "riots" of the 1980s. What we came across was inspirational grassroots projects that had helped St Paul's become a better place to live in during the intervening twenty-five years.

On the street with sex workers

The One25 Project works with women involved in prostitution, helping them to make positive choices about their lives. The project helps some of the most vulnerable young women in our society to escape from abuse and addiction. We heard several stories of young women sending cards of thanks, describing how their lives now involved stable, loving relationships.

Even lives that seem positive from the outside can so easily be destroyed. One young woman, whilst completing her "A" levels, became addicted to heroin. In order to feed her habit she began to work the streets, but now, thanks to the project, she had turned her life back on course.

Anne had a baby at the age of fifteen. Unfortunately, her relationship with her family broke down, resulting in her leaving home without her child. As with so many, a drug habit saw her dragged into the world of prostitution to pay for it, and a couple of spells at Her Majesty's pleasure followed. Eventually she met outreach workers from One25 on the street. Through a process of relationship building, and being encouraged and challenged about her life, she gradually came to see that things could be different. Not long ago the team were invited to a family party to celebrate her being reunited with her daughter and reconciled to her wider family, as well as being in a stable relationship and generally putting her life back together. At the party she remarked to the workers that Psalm 23 (which they had shared with her) was the thing that she held onto whilst in prison.

For us, it was great to be able to spend time with such committed people. The project was seeing real change, but change through pain and joy that involved the giving of oneself to serve the needs of others.

A few years before I had been asked to be Santa Claus at the Christmas party of this project, and I had written at that time:

> *I was dressed as Santa Claus once again and the sad thing is that I don't need the cushion to bolster up my tummy any more! It was a party for the children of some of the sex workers at the project. It's my favourite time of the year – the CEO gets a chance to let his hair down (what's left of it!), face-paint the kids, do the amateur dramatics (ho ho ho!) and facilitate the parachute games!*
>
> *As I came down the stairs of the project in my red garments (with accompanying false beard which, I soon discovered, I was allergic to!), I found myself surrounded by a group of working women. Before I could stop myself, I slipped into Santa mode, opened my mouth and promptly put my foot in it! "Have you all*

been good girls this year, then?" I said it before realizing what a naff thing it was to say to a group of women who must be so tired of the moral indignation that they so often suffer on the streets and in wider society. Thankfully, one of the girls saved me by taking the comment in the good spirit in which it was intended, and told me that if I let her sit on my lap she would show me how good she was! I can't think what she meant...

I reflected on this encounter as I was painting the face of one of the children later. I was sat in the corner of the room by the Christmas tree. On the sofa beside me was one of the other working girls, who had over-done the crack cocaine that had her on such a short lead of spiralling dependence. "This is where I want to be," was what I was thinking. "I learn so much here. I feel part of this community. I love this, and yet I so quickly have to return to the world of managing, of emails, phone calls, organizing events, committees, reports, public relations, fund-raising, letters, blah blah blah..."

The youngster I was face-painting brought me back to myself:

"Can you make me into an angel, mister?"

"Well," I replied, "I don't know if I can, but I'll have a darn good try!"

That's what it's all about – being alongside people, growing together, listening, ensuring that the training, management, theories and theologies are rooted in the questions of the children and young people. After all, redemption ripped through the surface of time in the cry of a tiny child. Perhaps I need to listen to the cry more carefully.

A few questions for your own reflection

- How on earth do you manage the interface between the differing worlds that we frequent as youth and community workers?

- How do you sort out the performance indicators to measure the quality of your sense of humour?

- What self-assessment procedure do I go through to check out with the kids whether or not I was a decent Santa?

- What contemporary youth work theory was I drawing on in this work?

- Was there scope for another funding bid to get the work onto a better footing?

Other encounters on the road

Having finished reflecting on my Christmas experience, we walked on into the shopping centre to talk to two young lads sat in the centre of The Mall. They were rolling cigarettes when we asked for their help. We explained our intentions – only this time, rather than looking for a "story of hope", we began by asking how they think young people are portrayed in the media. Their response was sophisticated and well thought through. No trite, shallow or defensive analysis, but rather, a clear concern that, yes, some young people are a problem. Many of them do get into trouble, but not all who wear hoodies are the spawn of the devil!

Both lads had been to a local university. They knew the Bristol night life well and were familiar with the local subculture. They were aware that they can sometimes seem intimidating, but they were proud of their friends and spoke warmly of them. We chatted about terrorism and the generalizations and stereotypes that run the risk of becoming self-fulfilling prophecies, hardening attitudes between faith groups and races. In a similar way, generalizations across the generations perpetuate barriers and divisions. One of the young men mentioned how his mother spoke highly of a mate of his who had helped her with her shopping the other day. However, we all agreed that this was less likely to make the news than the negative diet that the media markets so successfully. We said goodbye, and the lads shook our hands and wished us well.

After this we chatted with a group of skaters, and one young man in particular was eager to share his perceptions.

"I come to skate every day. If I miss a day, I feel that something is missing."

He had a lot to share about how he and other skaters were perceived by others. His premise was that the people who saw them skating in the park thought they were either up to no good or should have something better to do with their time. When asked about this perception, we got a surprisingly passionate response. Skating is actually quite a "polite" pastime. He said that while there tend to be quite a lot of young people hanging out and skating on the green, they are very aware of other people walking through that area and always make every endeavour to get out of the way. He told one story to illustrate the response he often gets. He fell down in front of one woman and so apologized for getting in her way. Instead of accepting his apology, all she seemed to see and think was that he was doing something pointless.

Another story he recounted was about him skating in the street. He was accosted by someone who told him it was dangerous. His perception was that it was on a long, straight street with very few cars. The cars could be seen from a long way away and they travelled very slowly. She told him that he should do something "useful" with his life, portraying him as a layabout, a good-for-nothing.

He politely pointed out that firstly, he was still in education and so was actually doing something with his life. Secondly, he asked if perhaps there were some other things she would like him to do with his time, such as drinking in the park, robbing her house or bullying her children. Instead, he had a hobby that kept him fit, and a community of peers who all looked out for each other. He even mentored younger kids in both the skills and decorum of skating. In skating there is a culture of the older ones being a role model for the younger ones.

As we sat, he pointed out that he knew everybody there, and some had become close friends, even though they were from different backgrounds and cultures. His observation was that this was how hobbies worked for most people, including adults. We asked him what the woman's response was. He shrugged – she didn't really say anything. How hard it seems for us adults to apologize to young people, even though we often stigmatize and stereotype them.

Then he came out with one of the most profound observations: "I reckon adults have a go at us because we have something they don't have." We think he meant "a life" but didn't quite say that. Instead he said he had found a hobby that he enjoyed, he got to meet people and make friends. He felt he did something that kept him healthy and, in particular, was part of a global community where he could go anywhere in the world and he'd have friends and even places to stay, despite cultural and social differences and barriers.

> "I reckon adults have a go at us because we have something they don't have."

It sounded like the ideal church to us! We felt that we had encountered a prophetic message to our own sense of "adulthood", where we often forget some of the things that make life, life. He enjoyed the counter-cultural elements of skating, that it was something other than mainstream, a place where you could be yourself and belong.

The following day we hitched to Cardiff and walked to Cardiff Bay and enjoyed the sun on the sea. After visiting a local youth work project, we wandered around Bute, an area of the city that is on the edge of the impressive dock developments. However, it's also an area that has something of a reputation for social issues. The area has a large Somali population, and we enjoyed some banter with local youngsters as we hung around.

The two white lads on the astro-turf pitch were hammering the ball from end to end of the multi-purpose football/basket-ball court, when we said hello and introduced ourselves as Welsh talent scouts! They laughed and carried on blasting each other. Chatting to them about what we were up to, we found the same willingness to talk and the same interest in our journey. The lads felt that the greatest sign of hope for them was the pitch they were playing on. They didn't feel particularly well connected to the Cardiff Bay success story, but were glad of the employment it had brought. They said that they liked their community, other than the ****s who had set fire to one part of the astro-turf. They felt that there was a good deal of harmony between the local white and black populations.

On the way out of Bute we met two Somali lads. The first lad was sat on his car smoking a joint; he was friendly and keen to help us when we asked for help, even before he knew what we wanted! This remains our experience; young people are willing to give time, to listen and to share. Bute has three of the highest indicators of social need in Wales and it has a reputation that goes back to the "fearful" days of Tiger Bay.

However, the first young man we spoke with was proud of his area and made a great offer to us and to anyone: "People who say bad things about this place should come and live here. They should visit us for about a week before saying anything about us." We thought this was a great idea and would like to say to any politicians or opinion formers that we will take them on a journey like this if they are interested!

We then spoke with the other young man, who was fiercely proud of the area in terms of its history, diverse culture and friendliness. He said that he never wanted to live anywhere else and had been in Bute for all of his twenty years. He was passionate about the community spirit, the carnival and his home. We were also surprised to some extent at the depth of his social analysis as he chastised those who wrote young people off, saying how he felt that young people would respond to negative labels and attitudes by fulfilling those expectations. Having developed something of a good relationship in such a short time, we shook hands and said our farewells. We reflected that either of these lads would have welcomed us into their homes to stay.

Skaters and Muslims

We managed to get lifts (some very exciting!) to Birmingham, and we wandered up to Victoria Square, having heard that it was the place in the middle of the city where young people could be found. We saw a group of three skaters who were very willing to talk to us and show us their moves. We had to look away a couple of times, as they attempted seemingly impossible tricks! Immediately we were struck by how polite they were, despite the stares and glares they were getting from passers-by. They were keen to stress that they had no desire to offend people but felt stigmatized by adults and even by other young people. One lad in particular told us about how he had been permanently excluded from school due to mental health problems, yet found a sense of freedom, creativity, excitement and achievement in his skating.

As with other stories, we were struck by how much young people appreciated having a couple of adults take an interest in them, their lives, experiences and stories. As we said we needed to move on, they urged us to watch one last trick. One lad in particular was determined to "land" (a technical term for success) a particularly difficult trick and proceeded to do so, with his final attempt in front of us. They seemed genuinely bemused by the idea that they might be a threat to society, simply wanting somewhere to express themselves and be with their mates. We were struck by their creativity, turning everyday objects into challenges just by using their imagination. Where we might have expected old-fashioned male pride and bragging, we found mutual support, care and encouragement. When he landed his final trick in front of us, boards were banged in appreciation. We left with a slight degree of envy that we didn't always find such support and camaraderie in our own lives. "You can't let your mates down" was their philosophy of life. This challenges our individualism, insularity and selfishness.

They seemed genuinely bemused by the idea that they might be a threat to society...

After someone kindly bought us a cup of coffee and a sandwich (amazing how we were looked after!), we walked on towards the main library. On the way we talked to two young Muslim men who were deep in conversation. Apologizing for interrupting, we explained our journey and asked them about hope and young people. To them hope came from Allah, from God. On hearing that we were Christians, they became quite animated, but not in the way our stereotypes might suggest. To them, everyone – Christians, Muslims and Jews – came from the same God. Rather than trying to convert us, they said we should each immerse ourselves in our religion to both understand it and live it. Hope, for them, was linked to peace. As far as they were concerned, we were each part of a peaceful religion. They saw common cause for concern in people misunderstanding and misrepresenting religious faith and its importance. They also felt that many involved in our respective faith traditions had not understood the basis of peace that ran through them.

One of them spent much of his time encouraging his peers to seek the wisdom of elders, to understand their faith, which far from radicalizing them, would actually enable them to live out the religion of peace properly. He did challenge us to read the Koran, to see what its actual message is rather than the distortions that they suggested existed. He also felt that the media had a responsibility both with regard to hatred of Muslims and their radicalization. They felt that the wider British population needed to realize that not all Muslims were the same. Just as Christians had their extremist elements and differing denominational perspectives, so did Islam. He suggested that many extremist positions in Islam did not understand Islam properly or were using it for their own ends.

To meet two young men who took their faith seriously, but not uncritically, and who encouraged us to do the same, was a great experience. As we were about to take our leave, expressing our thanks for letting us interrupt their conversation, they shook our hands and thanked us for all we were doing to overcome barriers and for really listening to what was being said. It certainly was a source of hope for us that genuine encounters of respect like this, without trying to dumb down some of the problems between our faiths, were possible. The hope was expressed in mutual respect and tolerance that was not ashamed of the importance of our own faiths, our traditions and our scriptures.

Social drama

We noticed six lads in hoodies and baseball caps looking around on the steps. Four of the boys were using their phones to video a staged fight between two of the lads. The white lad had a sling on whilst the black lad attacked. Suddenly the sling came off and the white guy turned the tables and fought back.

We approached the lads with the kind of trepidation that many of the adults around Victoria Square were probably experiencing as they watched the drama unfold, but these youngsters welcomed our interest in them.

> *We approached the lads with the kind of trepidation that many of the adults around Victoria Square were probably experiencing as they watched the drama unfold, but these youngsters welcomed our interest in them.*

We asked the lads for a few minutes of their time, to listen to them. The angle we took in our conversation was, "Don't you think that some of the adults around here will find what you're doing a bit scary? Do you think adults might get a bit scared of you guys? After all, you're wearing hoodies and caps."

The response was quick and unanimous: "That's because they never talk to us. We just want to have fun. We're not hurting anyone, are we? Even you were laughing!"

They were soon off again, pretending to drown each other in the local fountain! Actually, when I looked around Victoria Square, some of the adults were actually smiling at the lads. Hope?

Later on we went to a youth club on the edge of Birmingham where we let our hair down (well, what we have of it!) by playing pool, table-tennis and football with the local young people. It wasn't long before we were sharing our adventure and the young people began to open up about their own experiences. Gangs are the order of the day in Handsworth, and they are divided and labelled by postcode. The young people, that we felt honoured to meet, were part of B21. We asked them how they saw the gangs, on the basis that many adults would be fearful of them and newspapers would be very negative about guns, hoodies, fights, knives and so on.

The young people were not naïve or defensive about the way they were seen. They were aware of bad things that happened, but stressed that adults needed to talk to them rather than write them off. They felt that the gangs offered them safety and a sense of belonging and that they were close friends. It was very moving for me that the young people were very interested to hear about my own involvement in gangs – I (Dave) used to shave my head and engage in racial violence. They were also interested in my reflections on the dangers of racial separation and segregation that I had come across in South Africa during the years of apartheid.

Later that night the young people presented us with what they had been cooking – a huge bag of chocolate cakes for the journey! We were moved to tears.

Some further thinking, reflection and stories

I have always been fascinated by the way that we form our view of the world. One of my favourite cartoons has two men in the desert with a glass in front of them, with the caption, "The water evaporated before Doug and Fred could decide if the glass was half empty or half full." We are not born with a world-view; it is developed through a complex array of phenomena: culture, social conditioning, family values, nationalistic dogma, media propaganda, our need to please our friends, education, religion, politics and so on. Independent thinking may be a fine aspiration, but an honest exploration of our own thought processes and patterns is likely to lead to the conclusion that it is a myth. Are "immigrants" the threat to national security that they are often implied to be? Are young people all the yobs, thugs and vandals that the headlines so often depict them as? Are all football supporters "hooligans"? Are *Daily Mail* readers really fascists?

Is it a human race or a race for humans?

Our ability to generalize and speculate is a gift that enables us to attribute meaning, form opinions and speculate about the world around us. However, this ability also has the capacity to foster dogma, misunderstanding and fear. Young people get a bad press,[12] and I see no need for us to put up with such misleading generalizations. Many of us work and operate in ways that take us away from face-to-face contact with young people. Our attention and activities are dominated by thousands of perfectly reasonable organizational needs, busy schedules dictate our priorities, and a multiplicity of differing demands crave our attention and lay claim to priority in our lives. At times it can feel like the human race is just that – a wild chase to the elusive finishing line! I would want to argue that time spent listening to ordinary people, young people in particular, is critical to maintain some sense of balance in professional, personal and spiritual life.

Interpersonal contemplation and taking the risk

This kind of "interpersonal contemplation", as described in this chapter, has helped me to be clear about beliefs, has inspired my efforts as a leader and has shaped my understanding of personal and organizational priorities. Reflective theological discourse on the road, with people, is a must! Personal faith often runs the risk of becoming somewhat pedestrian, and it has been so good for me to prioritize a time to stop, listen and go out on the occasional limb.

> "Come to the edge," he said. They said, "We are afraid." "Come to the edge," he said. They came. He pushed them... And they flew.
>
> Guillaume Apollinaire

Going out on a limb might enable us to learn how to fly!

There is a real danger that our faith becomes a comfortably numb experience, one in which the red-blooded passion that God has for the world is expressed through tame traditions and shallow attempts at mission. Attempts at mission which will barely satisfy our own unconscious need for philanthropy, let alone respond to the pain of our world. Perhaps we are seduced into a world-view that has confused the temporal with the eternal, where our comfort and safety lure us into the protective cocoon of a faith; a faith that is characterized by stunted growth rather than the expansive inspiration of men and women like Dr Martin Luther King, Nelson Mandela and Mother Teresa, who said, "The fruit of faith is love and the fruit of love is service."

I believe that the insight and prophetic challenge offered by David Wells has to be heard and addressed by the church in the West if we are to rediscover the vibrancy and relevance of our faith. He said: "We have turned to a God we can use rather than to a God we must obey; we have turned to a God who will fulfill our needs rather than to a God before whom we must surrender our rights to ourselves."[13] I am convinced that even the most tentative exploration of what I call "interpersonal contemplation" will help free us from the tedium of a tame faith; it will liberate us from vain tradition and could well renew a passion for our fallen planet. This will of course involve a degree of risk, and the following story is a good cautionary tale:

> *A certain flock of geese lived together in a barnyard with great high walls around it. Because the corn was good and the barnyard was secure, these geese would never take a risk. One day a philosopher goose came among them. He was a very good philosopher and every week they listened quietly and attentively to his learned discourse. "My fellow travellers on the way of life", he would say, "can you seriously imagine that this barnyard, with great high walls around it, is all there is to existence?*
>
> *"I tell you, there is another and a greater world outside, a world of which we are only dimly aware. Our forefathers knew of this outside world. For did they not stretch their wings and fly across the trackless wastes of desert and ocean, of green valley and wooded hill? But alas, here we remain in this barnyard, our wings folded and tucked into our sides, as we are content to puddle in the mud, never lifting our eyes to the heavens which should be our home."*
>
> *These geese thought that this was very fine lecturing. "How poetical," they thought. "How profoundly existential. What a flawless summary of the mystery of existence." Often the philosopher spoke of the advantages of flight, calling on the geese to be what they were. After all, they had wings, he pointed out. What were the wings for, but to fly with? Often he reflected on the beauty and wonder of life*

outside the barnyard, and the freedom of the skies.

And every week the geese were uplifted, inspired, moved by the philosopher's message. They hung on his every word. They devoted hours, weeks, and months to a thoroughgoing analysis and critical evaluation of his doctrines. They produced learned treatises on the ethical and spiritual implication of flight. All this they did. But one thing they never did. They did not fly! For the corn was good, and the barnyard was secure.

M. Ridell, Threshold of the Future[14]

Perhaps the key question we face in our love for God and humanity is, Do we have the boldness of the likes of Jim Elliot, who said, not long before he was martyred, "He is no fool who gives what he cannot keep for that which he cannot lose"?

A few questions for your own reflection

- What do you think of the concept of "interpersonal contemplation"?

- How might it work for you?

- What would you do to apply it in your own life?

- What might be holding you back?

- Write out a plan to engage in active listening to others. Carry out your plan and then spend time reflecting on what you believe God has said to you through the process.

- What do you think about risk-taking in your faith?

- How does you faith feel just now? Have you become complacent at all? Do you need more risk?

- If you were to take a faith-based risk, what might it look like?

Story from the Edge 22:
Dave Wiles

As we approached a park on the edge of the city, I noticed a group of young people. They were the "types" that should be avoided! We approached the lads, who were drinking lager, smoking dope, spitting at anything that moved and generally exploring their identity in relation to loud music and fast cars. We needed their help. I asked them where they would sleep if they were sleeping rough that night, which turned out to be a great conversation starter: "Who are you?" "What is a pilgrimage?" "What is a Christian?" "Why does God let bad stuff happen?"

I wrote the paragraph above after a friend and I decided to go on a three-day pilgrimage (or retreat), carrying no money or equipment, but trusting that "all would be well" as we stepped out in faith. (This is not the same pilgrimage as the one mentioned earlier in this chapter.) We ended up having an extensive impromptu faith debate with the boys. The lads were great. They gave us careful advice about where to sleep, and where we should avoid, and they were quite concerned about our well-being, even offering us some of their cannabis! They also worried about how we would stay warm during the night, especially when they heard that we had no belongings, not even matches. One of them gave me his lighter straight away. Another grabbed some dry paper from his car, as it had rained and he was worried that we might not get a fire going.

Then my chin nearly hit the floor when they asked us to pray for them. So we asked God's blessing on the lads, especially hoping that they would stay out of any "scrapes" that seemed to have a strong chance of coming their way.

I was struck by several things as we walked on to their suggested location for the night – the local cemetery! Firstly, I was so encouraged that altruism seemed alive and well. Contrary to the populist dogma that young people are selfish and hedonistic, it was such a blessing to receive that young lad's lighter. The stark irony for me was that inscribed on the side of the lighter, in bold red letters, was the slogan, "THIS IS MY F***ING LIGHTER"!

Secondly, I realized that the whole event, in terms of it being a mission experience with them, would never have happened had we not started with our own need. So often "mission" seems all too ready to provide answers to questions that no one is asking, or to foist colonial-type help upon unsuspecting "natives". It occurred to me that Jesus met with the woman at Samaria with the request, "Please give me a drink"; he started his mission in Samaria with his need.

His incarnation was a similar expression of need; it was utter dependence upon a race that he later chose to die for. We talk about "incarnational youth work" in Christian youth work circles, and it seems to me that an important aspect of incarnation is honest recognition that we have needs too and that young people have so much to give us and teach us. Let us not forget that *we* may experience mission *from* young people – it's not necessarily always the other way round.

A few questions for your own reflection

- How have young people surprised you? How have they broken some of the stereotypes about them?

- What do you need from the young people you work with? How and when is it appropriate to ask for their help?

- What about incarnational youth work – does it fit with your experience?

- What model or models of youth work are you working on?

- What about a retreat for you too?!

Story from the Edge 23:
Isla Horton

As I work with young people, I am accompanying them on a journey. As a youth worker wanting to see young people develop, I'm pretty comfortable with that idea. What is less comfortable is the idea that I am on a journey too and that I *need* to change and grow just as much, and that it is often the young people I work with who help me see this.

I have got to know Kelly (not her real name) over the eight months that she has been coming to our drop-in. She is twenty-one. She lives in my idea of hell. Her dad deals heroin from her house to a constant stream of addicts, who come in and out at any time of night. Kelly is also addicted to heroin. On a typical night she works from the street until 3 a.m., to make enough money to buy the heroin that her body demands. In the drop-in Kelly often talks about her two children, who have been taken into care. She misses them desperately and fantasizes about taking them on days out to the zoo.

One day, Kelly comes into the drop-in and says she's had enough of the house. She wants to get out – can I help? A new hostel catering for Kelly's needs has recently opened and I ask if she's interested. We do the paperwork and Kelly passes the interview and gets a place. She says she's excited about the hostel, and I arrange to pick her up and help her move in the next day.

The next day, Tuesday, comes and Kelly isn't in. I look for her around the area, but no one has seen her. On Wednesday Kelly turns up and says she had to do something yesterday. "I'll move in tomorrow" – but of course, tomorrow never happens. I feel frustrated. What did I do wrong? Why didn't she go? Everything was set up; she just had to take one step. It seemed so easy. But easy for who?

What I am slowly realizing is that getting out of prostitution is not nearly as straightforward as I had assumed. Politicians talk about "exiting from prostitution" as if you open a door and simply step out. There is an assumption that with a little support, you just find a decent place to live, get a place in detox, and rebuild your life. But this assumes that young women want change. Change means the physical pain of withdrawing from heroin, and the emotional pain that hits you when the numbing effects of heroin have worn off, such as facing up to a childhood of abuse and losing your children. Change means losing your community, because of course, when heroin is the centre of your life, the only people who really know you are the people that you score drugs from and use drugs with.

Sometime later Kelly says, "To tell you the truth, I'm scared to come off the drugs." I ask her if she wants to go out for lunch. We sit in the sunshine in the park and eat McDonalds. We don't talk about housing, or detox, or anything that funders would probably be interested in. We just sit together and Kelly chats away. A while ago I would have questioned whether this was the best use of my time with Kelly. Surely I should be challenging her and bringing up these issues? But she is not yet ready for change. Don't misunderstand me – Kelly does need all of these things, and of course it is my role to help her see for herself that they are not things to be feared, but wonderful opportunities. But I have to ask myself, do I spend time with Kelly because I want her to change, or do I want change for Kelly because I've spent time with her?

So Kelly has helped me on my journey. Despite my need to feel like a great action-hero youth worker, I can't make a person change. I can't make a young woman come out of prostitution. Interestingly, God can't either. That is to say, I think he chooses not to force change. Instead he gently draws young people towards himself, working alongside them and in them, through the Holy Spirit. Kelly has helped me understand that change starts from within a person, not with a person being placed in a changed situation. Without realizing it, she is echoing what Jesus said: "The kingdom of God is within you."

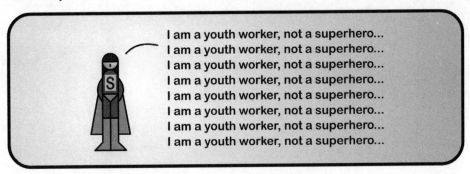

I am a youth worker, not a superhero...
I am a youth worker, not a superhero...
I am a youth worker, not a superhero...
I am a youth worker, not a superhero...
I am a youth worker, not a superhero...
I am a youth worker, not a superhero...
I am a youth worker, not a superhero...
I am a youth worker, not a superhero...

A few questions for your own reflection

- How do we take account of this aspect of youth work?

- How is your journey taking account of what you learn from young people?

- Can you identify the positive changes that young people have made to your Christian pilgrimage?

Story from the Edge 24:
Dave Wiles

I have recently returned to voluntary youth work involvement in a local authority club, where I started out my youth work training thirty-three years ago. I was a little taken aback in the team review after my first night, when one of the youth workers commented how good it was to have me there, relating to the young people as a type of grandfather figure! However, I know what he meant. It was great to be able to chat with young people whilst playing "Pass the Pig" without having to prove myself on the five-a-side pitch!

As I reflect on the night, I was struck by a few significant factors relating to the young people that I met. The young people were mostly aged between twelve and sixteen. The youth club is in an area of social housing, with quite high indicators of social deprivation. Of the thirty youngsters that I am beginning to get to know as I work in the club, I would say slightly more than half of them have been under the influence of a significant amount of alcohol or drugs whilst in the club each time I work there. This seems to me to be a higher percentage that my earlier days in youth work, and I believe it is of significant concern. It underlines the need for informal education around risk-taking behaviour and good informal social education. It also affirms the development of so many Street Pastor groups around the UK – people who are not moralizing and complaining about "binge drinking", but doing something positive as a response to it. All power and blessing to their elbows!

Another thing that struck me was the high numbers of young people who were unemployed, and I was well aware of the impact this was having on their use of time, their sense of self-worth and their ability to engage with the things that so many of us take for granted in society. Thirty-three years ago I was very involved in a host of differing responses to "youth unemployment" – some good and some not so good. However, it seems time to think again about how we can engage with employment issues with young people, especially those who are "vulnerable" or "at risk".

Bishop Roger Sainsbury writes:

In the 1970s, when I lived and worked in Canning Town, I wrote a booklet, Back on the Road to Wigan Pier, in which I shared some positive responses to a situation where in six years the local community lost 18,000 jobs. I introduced the booklet with a quote from George Orwell's Road to Wigan Pier (1937) – "lazy idle loafers on the dole" – as many were demonizing young people who were unemployed. The positive responses I shared were three Job Creation Projects our youth centre sponsored. The first employed twenty-five young people as farm supervisors to set up a farm in London Docklands; thirty years later it is still flourishing as Newham City Farm. The second was Newham Ferro-Cement Boats, building boats for youth and community projects; that scheme developed into Landmark Training, now seen as one of the best youth training projects in London. The third project placed nine young people as assistants in youth and community projects; I know one is now a lecturer at youth work college, another is a social worker and a third is a vicar. The objective of Job Creation schemes was "to prevent loss of familiarity with a working situation and help improve employment prospects." The jobs created were to be of "social value". Every day now I have been reading of major job losses in our newspapers. I am fearful again for the consequences for young people and I am asking, are we "Back Again on the Road to Wigan Pier"?

Perhaps some key questions for us as youth workers are:

- What are we doing to reduce risk and educate in relation to the use of alcohol and drugs?

- What is our response to increasing unemployment amongst young people?

- Will we still be going over these issues in another thirty-three years' time? How can we make a difference?

Story from the Edge 25:

John Walker

The front end of this project is a café selling tea and coffee and hot meals for homeless people. However, on Wednesday afternoons it isn't opened as a café, instead offering a time of church for the workers and clients together. All are welcome, though they are asked to be sympathetic to the service.

Around ten people were there this particular Wednesday, about a half-and-half mix of clients and staff. The service took the form of a few guitar-led songs and a short talk by the coffee-shop manager, plus some time for open prayer and response.

Ten minutes in, a regular client, Sandy, appeared at the door. He was smoking, which is fine, but what he was smoking smelt suspicious. After one of the staff explained that it was "church" this afternoon, he came in enthusiastically and sat down. It was pretty clear Sandy was smoking weed, and was soon asked to put it out. After a couple of songs, Sandy interjected and he began by telling us that he had just taken heroin, and had been on his way home to smoke some weed and relax, when he had felt that he should come into the café. He then told us about the time he had spent in prison, and his becoming a Christian there. He talked at great length, but with enormous passion, explaining how strongly he felt that Christ had guided him into the café that afternoon, and how much he wanted to change his life.

At the end of the time, we were to sing one final song. Sandy asked if we could sing, "Lord, I Lift Your Name on High". The leader said, "Yes, fine." Sandy then asked if he could play the guitar. The leader replied, "Can you play guitar?" Sandy confirmed that he could, and he was given the guitar, and he proceeded to make the most extraordinary sounds, intricate and alive, without written music. He led the singing – it was fantastic! As a group, we sat back and were stunned. Someone asked Sandy to keep playing, and he played his own improvised folk tunes while people cleared up.

My experience of church is very narrow. While I've been to a number of different denominational services, the majority of my experience has been in Anglican churches (albeit reasonably forward-thinking ones). I had

> *I had forgotten what church was. Church is two or three gathered in Christ's name.*

forgotten what church was. Church is two or three gathered in Christ's name. Church is a youth group. Church is Sunday morning with organs and dust. Church is heroin addicts and alcoholics gathered to worship God. I'd forgotten that.

Working with the homeless community, the cultural differences are as extraordinary as they are obvious. When working with a diametrically different culture, there comes the idea that I must have to, in some way, curb my middle-classness, adapt myself because I fear alienating someone, that I might be in some way offensive by my very me-ness.

And of course, the reality is that acceptance is done by the other person. Someone coming into a café to get their only hot meal of the week accepts me, as much as I accept them. I do not ask them to wear a top hat and carry a cane before I will serve them. (I don't wear a top hat, of course – it's impolite indoors!) To communicate cross-culturally, first an agreement of acceptance between the two cultures must be present. Otherwise, the communication is either dishonest (pretending to be other than you are), or not present.

A few questions for your own reflection

- How aware are we of our own culture and the way that can help or hinder our relationships in youth work?

- How "at home" are you with who you are?

- What is church, after all?

- What about the "old chestnut" of youth church? What are your views on this and other emerging forms of church?

- What bearing do your views have upon your relationships with young people or the church that you work for or attend?

Story from the Edge 26:

Dave Wiles

I still live a stone's throw from the council estate (called Southdown) that I grew up in and worked in for fifteen years as a youth and community worker. I have gone upmarket now and live in a private house, with a view! I'm still very much involved in the locality, as I am a volunteer youth worker in an adjoining estate; in fact, several of the youngsters in my current youth work are the offspring of youngsters that I used to work with in Southdown.

Just the other day I heard that one of the children of a young person that I used to work with is about to give birth – three generations of youth work! I still do "hatches, matches and dispatches" (dedications, weddings and funeral services) for local people. I see many of the youngsters that I used to work with as friends and neighbours, and there is a strong chance that I'll pop my own clogs here.

I have so many good memories of the youngsters we shared our lives with. Like Alex, who was so proud of his new leather jacket – on which he had displayed studs that spelt "Hell's Angles"! Or Derek, who tried to pierce my hand with a gardening fork when I had to take him home for fighting at club. Or Janet, who had two children before she was sixteen and still managed to come on our residential weekends in Devon to climb, surf and walk. Great kids who have all enriched my life and whom I still see around. So what has brought on this spurt of mid-life nostalgia, you may well ask.

Well... I've just been talking to a youth worker veteran who has spent the last few years in a youth work management post and he was wondering if he should have ever left youth work practice in his locality. Indeed, he even wondered if he had lost the path that was his faith journey, by being tempted away from direct work. I'm not sure if that is the case. I guess it's his question to answer. However, what we both agreed on was that long-term locally based youth work, work that is about long-term relationship formation with young people, is on the decline and has never really been appreciated for what it has achieved.

I must confess, it made me get out Bob Holman's book, *Kids At the Door Revisited*,[15] about the work that he and I did in Southdown. I wanted to reflect on what that work meant to some of the young people we had worked with, fifty-one of whom Bob interviewed for the book twenty years later. The quotes below confront the three-year-project mentality of so much contemporary youth work. They challenge fixed boundaries in relationships and underline the value of good preventative youth work, so I thought I would share a few of them and pose one or two questions for us as practitioners:

- "We felt part of it. I got on really well with the worker. It was like a big family. It made a lot of difference that the workers lived there... It gave us a sense of belonging."

- "They had a hard time looking after us and took a lot of stick from some of the boys... The leaders were all very down-to-earth and everyone got on so well."

- "They were approachable... you could talk to them and go to their house."

- "Without the project I would almost certainly have got into more trouble...What would have happened if I'd been sent down?"

When Bob checked the responses that he got from the fifty-one young people that he had interviewed, he noticed that there was a cluster of similar factors that they appreciated and identified about the youth workers. These were that the workers were: friendly (35 per cent of the fifty-one young people said this), approachable (20 per cent), trusted (18 per cent), lived locally (16 per cent), and were good organizers (12 per cent). Of the fifty-one young people, twenty-nine said that the clubs countered boredom and 21 said that the activities prevented them from getting into trouble (crime, vandalism, drug use etc.).

A few questions for your own reflection

- So are three-year projects as effective as this?

- What is to be gained/lost by living on the patch?

- Is it a nostalgic thing of the past?

- What about "professional boundaries"? How do such boundaries help/ hinder our youth work?

- Is your youth work "prevention" or "cure", and what's the difference?

Chapter 6

Sins and Blunders, and Other Thoughts on Spirituality

The other day I went to a local Christian bookstore and saw a "Honk if you love Jesus" car-bumper sticker. I was feeling particularly uplifted that day because I had just come from a thrilling praise service, followed by a thunderous prayer meeting, so I bought the sticker and put in on my bumper.

I was stopped at a red light at a busy intersection, just lost in thought about the wondrous meeting I had just come from, and I didn't notice that the light had changed. It was a good thing someone behind me loved Jesus too, because if he hadn't honked, I'd never have noticed the light. In fact, I found that *lots* of people behind me loved Jesus.

Why, even while I was still sitting there, the guy behind started honking like crazy, and leaned out of his window, screaming, "For the love of God, GO! GO!" What an amazing cheerleader for Jesus!

Then everyone started honking! I just leaned out of my window and started waving and smiling at all these loving people. I even honked my horn a few times to share in the love.

Then I saw another guy waving in a funny way with only his middle finger stuck up in the air. When I asked my teenage grandson in the back seat what that meant, he said that it was probably a Hawaiian good-luck sign or something. Well, I've never met anyone from Hawaii, so I leaned out the window and gave him the good-luck sign back. My grandson burst out laughing – why, even he was enjoying this religious experience!

A couple of the people were so caught up in the joy of the moment that they got out of their cars and started running towards me. I bet they wanted to pray or ask what church I attended, but it was then that I noticed the light had changed. So, I waved to all my sisters and brothers, grinning, and drove on through the intersection.

I noticed I was the only car that got through before the light changed again and I felt kind of sad that I had to leave them after all the love we had shared. So I slowed the car down, leaned out of the window and gave them all the Hawaiian good-luck sign one last time as I drove away. Praise the Lord for such wonderful folks!

Source unknown

I like the story above, as it is a good reminder that Christians get it wrong from time to time! It is so easy to get locked into a cloistered Christian world-view that has little or no relevance to the world around us. At times, it seems as if God requires his people to set the table for a dinner-feast that he has prepared for the world, and once the knives and forks have been neatly distributed, the church discovers that it is soup on the menu!

> *It is so easy to get locked into a cloistered Christian world-view that has little or no relevance to the world around us.*

I am not so sure that we humans have a God-shaped hole within us; I suspect it is a chasm! There were many reasons why I used drugs when growing up, but one powerful motivation was the struggle to find out who I was. Perhaps this is the meaning of spirituality – to find out where I, as a carbon-based being, connect to the rest of the universe and its Creator. I believe that the understandable location for our emotional and psychological sense of self is the internal world that, held captive by our five senses, is reaching for meaning in a universe that is full of juxtaposed fear and wonder. This is a journey which is characterized by exploration into the deep question, "Who am I?"

Spirituality – out of the body?

I was sixteen, and had left my body behind as I hovered across a great valley of crosses, the religious significance of the cross no doubt embedded in my psyche at Sunday school. As I flew through the valley, I could see in the distance a group of golden crosses that glowed luminously with beckoning warmth and significance. I could hear three voices, each discussing my future. One was arguing that my time was now and that I should be delivered up to an ending. The other argued that I had more to do on the earth and that it was not my time yet. The third voice decided that the second voice was correct, and I drifted back towards myself.

An overwhelming sense of oneness with the universe invaded my consciousness. I looked across at my arm and realized it was the spiralling star-system of a nebula that stretched to infinity across galaxies that I moved through with a heightened sense of awe and wonder. When I came back to myself I realized, with some embarrassment, that whilst travelling through space and time I had wet myself!

With fragile memories of the drug-induced trip across distant star-fields, I looked up from the pavement to see the police car driving by. I could see an officer peering at me as I hugged the gutter. It was LSD I had taken, and I found myself caught in a moment of time which repeated itself like a stuck video tape. I don't remember how many times I watched the patrol car travel past me, but when I came back to myself, I was in the police station, about to kick the policeman who was trying to get some sense out of me. As my leg and foot moved in a grand arch to connect with the officer's jaw, I became seduced by the strobe-like effect of my movements, and missed him by about ten seconds! He neatly folded me into a chair, realizing that I was no serious threat – just another hippy to plague his night shift.

Is there a ghost in the machine?

Whilst the psychology of my drug-induced experience is likely to be evident to anyone with even a basic understanding of the relationships between past experience and a slowly developing mind, I have to say I believe there is a "ghost in the machine". The rambling scenery of our subconscious mind accompanies our gathering momentum for some sense of rhyme and reason in life. I confess that I find myself with a default subjective position that my faith in God is of a similar nature to that of the man healed of his blindness by Jesus when he said, "I once was blind but now I see." My experience of God has led me to an unquestioning certainty about his existence and his presence in my life. However, I am happy to embrace the mystery that surrounds my certainty. I believe more and more about less and less, and whilst I know something about God, there is far more that I don't know; and whilst there is much I don't know about God, there is even more that I don't know I don't know! I am aware that my spirituality is a journey and not arrival, with more questions than answers.

There is much I don't know about God,
but there is much more that I don't know I don't know.

It is probably evident that I have considerable sympathy with a Christian mystic perspective on spirituality. To complete this spiritual disclosure, I should add that I have been profoundly moved and influenced by liberation theology[16] and the practices of community organizing.[17] With this in mind, I have come to the conclusion that perhaps the most powerful expressions of spiritual insight come from our own personal stories, from our understandings and experiences of Christ in the here and now.

Stories are the answer

Evident in my choice of title and material for this book is the belief that stories hold an intrinsic power to illuminate our journeys. I am less confident that sermons and large-scale missions hold the key to liberation. There is a greater power in the insight gained when people share the source of their hope, based on their stumbling discoveries and their personal pilgrimage and experience in "The Way".

As mentioned earlier, Peter challenges us to an authentic sharing of our spirituality when he asserts, "in your hearts set apart Christ as Lord. Always be prepared to give an answer to everyone who asks you to give the reason for the hope that you have. But do this with gentleness and respect, keeping a clear conscience" (1 Peter 3:15–16).

An interesting exercise to explore the power of personal story is to ask people to remember the three most significant sermons that have influenced their spiritual development and to think about the detail of those sermons. Then ask the same people to think of the three most significant people who have influenced their spirituality and why it is that those people have influenced them. Finally, ask those same people to compare and contrast the ease with which they were able to respond to the two parts of the exercise, and why this was so.

Usually it is people, not sermons, that impact our own spiritual growth most profoundly; often it is the quality of these relationships and the sharing of interpersonal stories that have the deepest impact. Having carried out the exercise above, I have discovered that many people cannot even recall one sermon that has impacted their spiritual development, whereas they are able to recall deep learning from relationships and shared stories with fellow pilgrims.

We are the good news! It is truth that sets people free, said Jesus (John 8:32). In the same way that Jesus offers us the insight that he, in person, is truth (John 14:6), so might we represent the truth as we share the hope he has provided. When I have managed to live by this understanding, I have always found that young people are interested.

Stories on the street

The belief that young people are still interested in spirituality, despite their absence from institutional church and organized religion, is always affirmed when I trawl the streets of my city as a Street Pastor. In fact, it was during a two-hour slot on the streets from 2 a.m. to 4 a.m. recently, that I approached Naomi and Sarah as they sat on a wall overlooking a park – some twenty feet below! I just wanted to make sure that they didn't fall. Anyway, they were quite sober and responded with a smile because I had cared enough to check them out. Which led on to a conversation about what a Street Pastor was, why we did it, and then a great discussion about things that mattered most in life. Naomi carried on chatting with me whilst

> *The belief that young people are still interested in spirituality... is always affirmed when I trawl the streets of my city as a Street Pastor.*

Sarah, inspired by the philosophy of Street Pastors, went to help a couple of girls who looked a bit vulnerable down the street. Naomi opened up an area of her past life that concerned her deeply – something that she was worried that neither she herself, nor God, would ever be able to forgive. We talked and I listened, and in the end, I think I was able to help her with the issue to the extent that she smiled, jumped off the wall and gave me a huge hug! I was very moved that here was a deep spiritual encounter at 2 a.m. in the morning that offered her enough hope to say that she might well give church a try again – she had given up on it six years ago. Naomi would not have darkened the door of any church and she, like most of her generation, is deeply interested in God (outside of organized religion). How do we reach this generation of young people (especially eighteen to twenty-five year-olds) through our youth work effectively?

It was later the same night that Frank approached us. He was slightly more than half cut and he looked very anxious and sounded quite depressed. I think it was the word "pastor" that attracted him to us, as he tentatively reached out to share the grief he felt at losing his dad a year ago. He had got "hammered" in the pub, trying to drown a sorrow that overwhelmed him, to the extent that the week before, he had tried to take his own life.

There are no quick-fix answers to grief (I recommend that you read *The Shack* by William P. Young if you want to explore the subject), so we offered a sympathetic ear and gave him some of what we could – our time. When he began berating himself that, at twenty, he had wasted his life, I decided it was appropriate to share some of my own story briefly. I mentioned how thirty-three years ago, at twenty, I had experienced a profound encounter with a God of love who turned my world upside down and then started me on what has been a fantastic adventure ever since.

He was interested and I sensed a lifting in his spirit as I asked him what he felt his dad would want for him. He smiled and replied that his dad would want him to be happy. We then discovered that his best friend was a friend of my family, and this really seemed to inspire him to think that our encounter was "ordained". I said, "Perhaps", and he joined us on the rest of our rounds.

Some further thinking, reflection and stories

In this chapter I have focused upon the formative aspects of an evolving spirituality and the place of sharing and hearing stories of hope. I have argued, like others,[18] that young people are spiritually awake and have a wide-eyed interest in spirituality, even if they are giving up on the institutional church. In this final section I will share a number of stories from my own experience that I believe offer important messages about God's heart for humanity.

I really, really like you

In the mid 1980s I was visiting a priest in the Bronx, New York. I must have looked like a naïve tourist as I emerged from the subway onto the streets, with suitcase in tow and map in hand. I must confess that I felt a bit nervous as I was offered drugs by a guy at the top of the subway steps. My nervousness increased as I looked at the fire-ravaged apartments. Many landlords were torching buildings in those days for insurance purposes. I was also a bit fazed by the razor-wire fences which were around the churches, and when I realized I was clearly a minority white face in a black community, I just felt intimidated – not that anyone had threatened me, I just felt insecure.

I had to catch a bus to Father Peter's church and so I asked a woman at the nearest bus stop if the number 46 stopped there. She replied that it did and I stood waiting for the bus with a growing sense of unease. One of those subliminal fears was upon me; I just felt that something was very wrong; the hairs on the back of my neck were electric and I felt paralyzed by anxiety. The daftest notion passed through my head – that this was the wrong bus stop. I was too self-conscious to ask the woman again and I had no way of doing anything about my fear, other than to pray, "Is this the right bus stop, God?" The prayer went through my mind before I could even rationalize that God might be a tad too busy with the grander schemes of the universe to take time to respond to my request for travel information updates!

Anyway, I wonder if you can imagine my shock when a disembodied voice (well, it came from a passing car, actually) shouted, "Hi, Dave! Are you going to Father Peter's home? If so, you are at the wrong bus stop. You need the one across the road that doesn't go out of town!" It was another priest whom I had met a long way away in Baltimore the week before, who happened to be passing when I was requesting help from God!

I thanked my Catholic angel and crossed the road in a daze. I was mulling over the significance of what happened as I waited for the bus. How come all my prayers don't elicit that kind of action and response from God? Was that for real? Why did it happen to me?

It was at this point that some verses from the Bible registered: "Are not two sparrows sold for a penny? Yet not one of them will fall to the ground apart from the will of your Father. And even the very hairs of your head are all numbered. So don't be afraid; you are worth more than many sparrows" (Matthew 10:29–31). I felt a still small voice in my mind suggesting that I was worth more than many sparrows!

As experiences in my spiritual life go, this felt like a mountain top to me. I would never dream of suggesting that it offers deep insight into the mysteries of prayer, nor that it was evidence of my faith – I know it wasn't. I, like so many Christians, am well acquainted with, and experienced in, the complexities and conundrums of unanswered prayer. Hundreds of Christians joined my family and I when my daughter was terribly ill for three years before we saw any progress. It would be such an insult to Christians in the developing world to imply that their plight was connected to a lack of faith in their prayer life in any way.

I believe now that I had this experience so that I could share the story (as I have done over several decades) with people who need to know that God is aware of, interested in and able to react (in his sovereignty) to the details and concerns of our daily experience. He really does know about the hairs on our head. He really is familiar with all our ways (Psalm 139), and I think he really, really likes us!

People matter

It was in the mid 1970s that I became a Christian, and I sometimes compare the experience to being immersed in what Douglas Adams (in *The Hitchhiker's*

Guide to the Galaxy) called "the Total Perspective Vortex" – a place where your perspective is suddenly opened to broader horizons. I am certainly not saying that everyone will have or has had as clear-cut an experience as I had in coming to faith. I think it was C. S. Lewis who said that his conversion to Christianity was intellectual and that he came into the kingdom of God kicking and struggling. Amazingly, it seems to me that God graciously meets people where they are. It was, like the apostle Paul, a "road to Damascus" experience for me, and my adolescent hedonism was suddenly relegated as I became aware of the needs (and even existence!) of other people.

So it was that I found myself looking at the council estate that I had grown up in and realizing that the environment that young people experience has a profound effect upon their life chances and life experiences. I thought about my own amateur approach to gardening and how often I left plants in pots that were far too small for them to grow. How stunted, pale and under-developed the plants looked in the wrong environment. It seemed to me that this was evidence for the damaging impact of nurture upon the fragility of nature. I believed that God cared about the environment that young people grew in, and instinctively I had not separated social concern from spirituality. Indeed, it was only some time later that I read these words by R. Bakke:

> *It is only in our rich Western countries that we have the luxury to divide two sides of a common coin – social action and evangelism. John Stott uses such images as the two belonging together like two blades of a pair of scissors or two wings of a bird. Christians who are still debating these priorities often miss the point that social action is not done in order to communicate the gospel, but as a sign or evidence that the gospel has already been received and acted*

upon. Social ministry is the loving service of Christians set free
from sins and bondage by the risen Lord.[19]

So it was that under a failing street-light, when I was sharing my new Christian story with local youngsters, many of whom were in awe of my sordid history, I prayed that God would intervene in my neighbourhood.

It was not long after this prayer that Dr Robert Holman (Bob) felt a Christian conviction that his seat as Professor of Social Policy at the University of Bath was not the vocation that God had intended for him. So he and his wonderful family left the suburbs and moved into my neighbourhood. I rejoiced and chalked up another answered prayer. However, little did I know or suspect that this was only one aspect of God's answer to my prayer. The next aspect came when Bob and I met – he believed that I was the answer to *his* prayer! My street credibility and natural relationship with young people was just the lever that he needed to launch his youth and community project, and so began a long story in which he and I, and so many people, discovered just how wonderful God's ways were in moving people to love and care for each other.

The ten years that we spent working together in Southdown have been well documented elsewhere.[20] However, in this book I just want to endorse the assertion that people matter to God. When we take steps, however hesitant and cautious, in the direction of joining in with God's love for the world, we discover he is there already and stays long after we have gone.

I also think that the characteristics of the Southdown Project are worth noting for consideration in our plans and projects in the twenty-first century. In summary, they were:

- A belief that local people have the skills and ability to respond to their own concerns. I was described as an indigenous worker (native) who became a "new careerist". However, I would want to argue that there were many young people in that neighbourhood who could have done what I did – indeed, others did become involved.

- That a dedicated facilitator and mentor like Bob Holman is key to the success of local project work. Whilst I know that Bob would understate his own involvement and leadership of the Southdown Project, I know it would never have worked without him.

- A commitment to reciprocity and mutuality of relationships; being able to give and take in caring relationships. Perhaps this is a characteristic that calls into question the professionalization of human services.

- That living in the area in which one carries out youth and community work may well be demanding and challenging, but it certainly increases the chances that you are available at the point and time of need. Also, your perspective is rooted in, and able to use, the natural and local support networks that, at the end of the day, are what people really rely on when times are tough.

- That friendship with the people you work with is not necessarily an objective of your youth and community work, but something that occurs and can strengthen your efforts to carry it out. I still live on the edge of Southdown (some thirty years after the project was started) and am honoured that I frequently (as mentioned earlier) carry out "matches", "hatches" and, sadly, "dispatches" for generations of the people that some would suggest I "worked with".

We are partners with God

As I sat drinking my cocoa, whilst looking out across the amazing hills in the West of Scotland, I had a rare moment of honest humility when I prayed along the lines of, "God, this is amazing! You made all of this! You don't need me at all, do you!" Whether it was my imagination, or the still small voice of God, or both (!), I don't know, but in my mind I heard a response: 'Yes, you're right – I don't need you... but I do *want* you!" It was a timely reminder for me that I am a partner with God. A junior partner – but definitely a partner!

I think it would be appropriate to end a book about "Stories from the Edge" with a few final stories. I would like to leave you with both a sense of encouragement and something of a challenge to carry with you in your own *partnership* with God.

Firstly, a story that celebrates the notion that we are junior partners and that God seems to thrive in transforming our weakness into his strength,

our darkness into his light, and our failure into his redemptive success...

A water-bearer in India had two large pots, both hung on the ends of a pole which he carried across his neck. One of the pots had a crack in it while the other pot was perfect and always delivered a full portion of water. At the end of the long walk from the stream to the house, the cracked pot arrived only half full. For a full two years this went on daily, with the bearer delivering only one and a half potfuls of water to his house.

Of course, the perfect pot was proud of its accomplishments. But the poor cracked pot was ashamed of its own imperfection, and miserable that it was able to accomplish only half of what it had been made to do. After two years of what it perceived to be a bitter failure, it spoke to the water-bearer one day by the stream:

"I am ashamed of myself, and I want to apologise to you. I have been able to deliver only half my load because this crack in my side causes water to leak out all the way back to your house. Because of my flaws, you have to do all of this work, and you don't get full value from your efforts," the pot said.

The bearer said to the pot, "Did you notice that there were flowers only on your side of the path, but not on the other pot's side? That's because I have always known about your flaw, and I planted flower seeds on your side of the path, and every day while we walk back, you've watered them. For two years I have been able to pick these beautiful flowers to decorate the table. Without you being just the way you are, there would not be this beauty to grace the house."

Secondly, here is a story that I heard many years ago that was offered to me as a way of understanding the difference between involvement and commitment.

> *The council of farm animals had met to discuss the forthcoming birthday of the farmer. The horse had called the meeting, as this year was of great significance in that it was the farmer's sixty-fifth birthday, "a year that the humans deem significant, for reasons best known themselves," he said.*
>
> *"Why don't we surprise him by mucking out the barns?" suggested the dog.*
>
> *"Or why not weed his garden?" suggested the sheep.*
>
> *"I know," said the goat. "He loves his full English breakfast – let's get him a year's supply."*
>
> *At which point the chickens all squawked, "What a great idea!"*
>
> *But the pig retorted, "Rubbish! You would only be involved in the breakfast, but I would be committed!"*

It seems wrong to be unclear about the cost of partnering with God through our commitment. However, it would be just as wrong not to underline the rewards of letting go of the things that hold us back from discovering that faith is spelt "R-I-S-K".

> *This story is about a man from Crete who loved his native isle. When he is dying, he has his sons carry him outside and lay him on the ground. At the moment of death, he reaches down and takes a handful of earth and dies a happy man.*
>
> *At the gates of Heaven, God comes out and invites the man in, but tells him he must first let go of the dirt he still holds. The man refuses, holding his fist shut tight.*
>
> *God goes back inside, sad. Years pass and God comes back outside the gates in the form of an old friend. They chat and quaff a beer, and God suggests it's time for them to enter the bounty of Heaven. The man starts in but God says he must let go of the dirt in his hand. Holding his fist shut tight, again the man refuses, and God goes back inside, sad.*

> *Eons go by, and the man gets older and older, arthritic and bent with age. God comes outside in the form of a little granddaughter who tells the man she is waiting for him. She pleads for him to come in and enter the bounty of Heaven. The man is very old and crippled. He agrees to enter but needs assistance. As he reaches to take the little girl's arm for support, his arthritic fingers open and the dirt slips through them.*
>
> *The man enters the gates of Heaven, and the first thing he sees is his beloved isle of Crete!*

At the end of the day, it seems to me that the challenge is to implement the radical calling and teaching that Jesus both lived and delivered, as we stumble forward seeking that his "kingdom come".

> *A man was lost in the desert, just dying for a drink. He stumbled upon an old, weather-beaten shack – ramshackle, windowless, roofless. He thought it would offer him nothing, but it gave him a little shade from the heat of the desert sun. Then he saw an old, rusty pump, ten or fifteen feet away. He stumbled over to it, grabbed the handle and began to pump, up and down, up and down. But nothing came out.*
>
> *Disappointed, he staggered back, and off to the side he saw an old jug. He looked at it, then wiped the dirt and dust off it, revealing a message which read, "Prime the pump with water, my friend, and fill the jug again before you leave. PS: you have to prime it with all the water."*
>
> *He popped the cork off and saw water. Now he was faced with a decision: if he drank the water he could live, for a little while at least. But if he poured all the water into the old, rusty pump, maybe it would yield fresh, cool water from the well deep below.*
>
> *He studied both options. What should he do? Pour it into the old pump and take the risk, or drink the jugful and stay alive for a while – but at the expense of those who might follow?*
>
> *He poured all the water into the pump, and he worked the handle – squeak, squeak, squeak. And nothing came out. He worked the handle again – squeak, squeak, squeak. Then a little drop began*

to come out, and then a little dribble, and finally out gushed fresh, cool water. He filled the jug and drank it, he filled another and drank it.

Then he remembered. He filled the jug to the top for the next traveller, then corked it. And he added this little note: "Believe me – it really works!"

You have to give it all away, before you can get anything back. That is the kingdom.

Finally, to challenge you and, I hope, to leave you with a smile, here is a slightly re-told story to inspire your efforts in partnering with God:

> *One night I had a wondrous dream,*
> *One set of footprints there was seen,*
> *The footprints of my precious Lord,*
> *But mine were not along the shore.*
>
> *But then some stranger's prints appeared,*
> *And I asked the Lord, "What have we here?*
> *Those prints are large and round and neat,*
> *But Lord, they are too big for feet."*
>
> *"My child," he said in sombre tones,*
> *"For miles I carried you alone.*
> *I challenged you to walk in faith,*
> *But you refused and made me wait.*
>
> *"Because in life, there comes a time,*
> *When one must fight, and one must climb,*
> *When one must rise and take a stand,*
> *Or leave one's butt-prints in the sand."*

Source unknown

A few questions for your own reflection

- What is the good news, according to you? If you were asked to explain what you hope for and why, what would you say?

- Do you have any evidence that young people are interested in spirituality? What is your evidence and how do you respond to this knowledge?

- Knowing that God likes you, as well as loves you, can be a liberating insight that radicalizes our world-view and actions. Do you believe it (and if so, why do you believe it)?

- How does your understanding of God impact your lifestyle and life choices?

- Why not write a letter to yourself as from God and post it to yourself in a week's time. You may find this encourages and challenges you.

- How is your partnership with God going? Is there scope to move on the spectrum of "involved" and "committed"? What would you do to make that happen?

Story from the Edge 27:

Dave Wiles

"I think Christians are a bunch of narrow-minded hypocrites!"

"What's wrong with sex before marriage?"

"Why can't I look at the witchcraft websites?"

"Who says it's wrong whacking someone if they're playing you up?"

The list of tricky questions that I have "fielded" in youth work situations seems endless. Not only do the young people test me, in terms of my own (and the church's) moral coherence, but the adults I talk to about youth work challenge me too!

"What do you mean, you give them condoms – doesn't that encourage promiscuity?"

"Surely if you give them needles for their heroin, you are only encouraging them?"

"Why do they behave so badly?"

"I blame the parents."

"If only they had more discipline."

Since when was the wisdom of Solomon a prerequisite on a youth worker's job description?!

Where do you draw the lines in terms of what you will and won't discuss with young people? A good example is the debate surrounding Harry Potter. I must confess that I worry that we ask the wrong questions in relation to some of the dilemmas we face about contemporary culture. In the case of Harry Potter, many of the questions we ask revolve around the issue of whether it is a morally "right" or "wrong" story for young people to access? Should we read or watch it? Will it influence young people in a negative way? This type of moral reductionism seems a bit like the question, "Is it right to play the lottery?" Surely a more important question for us, as Christians, is "Why do people get so much hope from the lottery?"

Too often, it seems that Christian debate is completely given over to questions of defining what is "right" and what is "wrong". Have we developed beyond the early Jewish Christians who kept hijacking God's grace with questions about the rights and wrongs of circumcision (see Galatians)? So many young people say to me that they couldn't get involved with church because they are not good enough. All the time that we Christians are straining to define rights and wrongs, we run the risk of putting yet more hurdles in front of young people and their potential experience of God.

In my youth group, and amongst the young people I meet, I have shared in some excellent discussions about Harry Potter as well as many other books, films and programmes. The list includes *The Matrix*, *The Lord of the Rings* (J.R.R. Tolkien), the *His Dark Materials* trilogy (Philip Pullman), the *Wind on Fire* series (William Nicholson), *Eastenders* and many others. These discussions have covered in some depth the themes of forgiveness, repentance, sacrifice and redemption, often in a spontaneous and authentic way that I could never have planned as a "lesson".

> *All the time that we Christians are straining to define rights and wrongs, we run the risk of putting yet more hurdles in front of young people and their potential experience of God.*

My question would be, how can we use contemporary interests/culture to enable young people to connect with God? Look at Paul on Mars Hill (Acts 17:16–34). Despite the fact that he was "upset to see all the idols" (verse 16), we read that he uses the contemporary context to connect with the people. Imagine if he had started his sermon with, "I found an idol to the Unknown God... You can't have idols, it's against the law!" or "This is theologically unacceptable" or "This could lead you into idol worship." No, instead Paul makes a connection with popular culture and goes on to share good news with the crowd in such a way that eventually they want to hear more.

A creative and moral test for Christian youth work is to enable young people to get beyond the almost Pavlovian guilt/defensiveness/fear reaction that so many have when anything to do with God is mentioned. This needs to be long enough for young people to catch on to the tenderness of God's mercy and love. At times this may demand that we bite our theologically correct tongues in order to explore spirituality in a non-defensive and open climate. Was James mostly worried about swearing when he wrote about the dangers of the tongue (James 3), or was he more worried about what we might do to each other with our sophisticated and elaborate moral language codes?

A few questions for your own reflection

- So where do we draw the line in discussions with young people?

- What are your moral absolutes – how do they affect your relationships with young people?

- How can we develop ways of connecting with contemporary culture so that we don't compromise our own belief systems?

- What books, films, plays, soap operas, poetry, TV programmes, YouTube videos and stories have you found useful in opening up God-talk with young people?

Story from the Edge 28:

Peter Hope

We never really planned it this way, but then the proverb about man planning and God deciding seems to be the most appropriate when it comes to describing Out4Good. Nobody likes to house persistent prolific offenders (PPO), especially when they are young and have accrued arrears from other accommodation and have most likely failed in every other area of housing. They are a big risk.

I don't know what the term "persistent prolific offender" conjures up in your mind's eye, but in mine it was *Bad News*! I believed that we certainly couldn't take the risk of giving them accommodation; what we needed were some success stories to convince funders and supporters about what a great job we were doing and what a difference we were making.

Thankfully, that judgmental and self-serving attitude has been blown out of the water, with God deciding something quite different. Four of the five lads we have housed since November 2007 fall into the PPO category.

I love them – they're great! All four of them have substance-misuse issues, borne out of emotional difficulties and the now-familiar statistic of an absent father at a crucial time in their lives. Of the twenty-four young men I have met in the project, I can tell you that not one has had a stable father figure in his life. That is not to say that every lad who has an absent father will turn to drugs and crime, but my stats make stark reading on that front.

Why do I love them? Well, it's not the chaotic lifestyles that they can bring or their behaviour – I am still challenged on that one. But each has shown me something of the grace of God in our lives; I get a fuller understanding of that every day. And in all honesty, it was the lad who was not a PPO, and who hadn't been in prison, and who didn't have a drug habit, unlike the other four, who presented the greatest challenges and actually stole from the project, and even abandoned his room. On the face of it, he was the one who should have been the "success", going to college and so on. The other four have already been written off by society.

I know it is unwise to look at it in terms of "success" and "failure", but on the face of it, things look to be on the failing side. The average stay for the lads in the house is around three months. That isn't by design – that's how it's working out. It is a nightmare in Housing Benefit (HB), as that is the only money we receive to offset the cost of the rent on the property. We fall well short at the end of each month. It costs the project £1,000 per month in rent and bills, and HB returns around £500. It's a good job we have an understanding landlord who is a supporter of Frontier Youth Trust! However, we need to see the financial structure becoming much more secure to ensure the continuation of the accommodation.

The lads move on for a variety of reasons, but a major one is the failure to get work, and they give up. Living on benefits is not the life of Riley depicted by the right-wing press. They just want a decent wage, but cannot get it. However, they can "earn" quite well out of other activities, so rather than compromise the values of the house, they move on.

Why are we different to other charities that offer accommodation to ex-offenders? Well, the reality is that there aren't that many who are doing it. The difference with Out4Good is that it is low-occupancy accommodation, we will accommodate PPOs, and we have "live in" support.

Two young lads share the house with a live-in "lead tenant", currently a man called Pat who is from the Congo – a displaced person himself. Pat has a serving heart for these youngsters. He helps looks after them, and he has a pastoral role with them. Other mentors are also involved, and there is a welcoming Christian community for the lads to integrate into if they so wish. The next challenge for the community to come up with is a well-founded business plan that can give the lads a good opportunity for paid employment. It is the one vital part of the jigsaw that is missing at the moment.

All the lads have the opportunity to join in prayer, Alpha groups, football, and communal meals. The two current lads are fully engaging with all that the community can offer. Support is given in applications for benefits, developing life skills, registering with doctors, applications for jobs and college courses, family liaison – and basically, we share our lives with them.

Finally, to further dispel the myth that PPOs are an impossibly high risk to house, that they will smash the house up, not look after it, have a stream of dubious guests, deal drugs and so on, I can say our experience has been to the contrary. Yes, we have had issues – but then, if you rented your house to students, you would find the same issues. But because we have someone at hand as a "live in" lead tenant, situations come to light quickly and can be dealt with more efficiently. We have also nurtured a good relationship with other agencies in the area working with young people who have offended – for example, the Youth Offending Team, the police, drug agencies and so on.

The two lads in the house at the moment do their own shopping (legally!), cook their own food, clean up after themselves and do the gardening. One of the lads has never done anything in a garden before, but now we have a flourishing vegetable patch. His comments on watching the plants grow and comparing that to his growth in faith were the most profound I have heard from any young person – let alone a young offender. They are fastidious in personal hygiene, are respectful and considerate around the house, and want to pay their way. Compare that to the average nineteen-year-old lad, and these boys are saints! The trouble is that they just keep making poor choices and – oh yes! – they keep getting caught.

> *They are not inherently bad; they have just made poor choices through a variety of circumstances.*

Persistent Prolific Offenders are no different to you and me. They are not inherently *bad*; they have just made poor choices through a variety of circumstances. Yes, they do things we would call bad, but perhaps if we were openly labelled "Persistent Prolific Sinners", we would be more inclined to empathize with these lads and do something constructive about their situation. If there were to be a legacy that Out4Good could offer these lads, it would be to see them understand the *good news*. I want them to know the potential that they have. Oh, and I would also like to see the wider Christian community fully mobilized, radical and committed to this kind of work.

A few questions for your own reflection

- What about the PPOs in the area where you are working - are you connecting with them?

- Should you think about it?

- How would you go about it?

Story from the Edge 29:

Jo Fitzsimmons

Sexually Transmitted Diseases (STDs) seem to be a fascination of my group. I'm not sure why, but it takes up a lot of talk time with our hoodie-wearing, ASBO-competing teenagers.

There is only so much you can listen to in detail about STDs without feeling queasy, and spending yet another Sunday evening discussing them wasn't in my original strategy for working with this group from our estate. I walked around to the meeting wondering if I was going to be able to endure the evening, and pleading with God for us to be able to share something of hope for a group of kids for whom the upcoming Christmas wasn't going to be a lot of fun.

That evening proved me wrong – yet again! Only three lads showed up – most of the others had been grounded, or banned, for various pre-Christmas antics. So when the lads walked in we settled into the usual hot-chocolate-and-toast routine and conversation. Or so we thought.

The smaller group meant the lads seemed more open. James, who we had known for four years, started chatting about how his mum had nearly lost her baby because she'd got into a fight with his aunt, the local drugs dealer, and it was touch and go if the baby would live. He told us he had asked God to make the baby OK. The baby survived and his mum was doing well. This opened up conversation about other times they'd prayed. How did God hear them? Was it OK to ask God to help them "batter" bad people? Stories of "deals" they'd done with God came out – for example, "God, if you help get me out of this, I'll stop smoking weed for a week." And what did they think God would do if they didn't keep up their end of the "deal"?

After half an hour of the stories and questions about praying, we asked them if they wanted to write down some things we could pray for them. "Why can't we pray now instead?" James asked. So we spoke briefly about what they wanted to ask God for and then, as we were just about to pray, one of the lads shouted "*Stop!*"

We all looked at him. I felt he was either going to tell us it was all rubbish or be angry, feeling he had been pressured into praying when he really didn't want to and we were "Bible bashing" him. Wrong again, Jo! I guess God smiled at me. "We haven't asked you what we can pray about for you," he said.

I told them of a family situation that was deeply difficult for me. My colleague told them about her husband who had been ill. So we all prayed together. Rough, simple, no jargon – short calls for God to listen to a bunch of lads with ASBOs, who wanted to know that he would hear them and help them.

Are they changed young people because of this situation? Have they stopped smoking weed? Are they now out of trouble? Nope, but I have no doubt they experienced something of the outcast boy, born in a barn, with a bleak future ahead of him. And I guess they know that he'll listen when no one else at school, at home, in the Job Centre, seems to hear their voices.

And me? I *was* changed. God became bigger, as I yet again realized that participation was as much about me participating in what God is already doing as it was about young people choosing to participate in their youth club, community and world. Also STDs don't seem too bad any longer!

A few questions for your own reflection

- Are we prepared for God to challenge us about our presumptions and assumptions?

- Do we take the challenge of asking our young people to pray with us/ for us?

- How do we help young people to participate in prayer and relate it to their lives?

Story from the Edge 30:

Dave Wiles with Paul Hazelden

I was both moved and challenged by these words, from a project in Bristol that FYT supports:

Who speaks for the voiceless? Who speaks for the weak, the poor, the vulnerable, the oppressed, the powerless, the cold, the hungry and the despised? Who speaks for those who do not know what they need, because they have never had it? For those who do not know the right words to use? For those who do not have the right to speak? Who speaks for the voiceless? Not me. Even to attempt to speak for the voiceless is to deny who they are. They have no voice. They cannot speak. And they cannot speak through the mouths of well-meaning, powerful, articulate people. I cannot speak for them because they cannot speak. Even to attempt to speak for the voiceless would be to deny who I am. I am not voiceless. Compared to them, I am rich and powerful. I cannot speak for them because I am not them, I do not know what to say. I must not pretend that I know, that I understand. I have not stood where they stand. I have not been ignored, overlooked and forgotten. I cannot speak for them, but I can remember that we have met. Our paths crossed, and I have been changed by that meeting. I do not know their experience; I do not understand their dreams and fears. But neither am I completely ignorant: we met, and I learned one thing at least. They are people like me. I do not need to speak for them. But I must speak, knowing they are present. I must allow them to shape my words, my work and my world. I cannot pretend that the voiceless do not exist. The future I strive to build must have a place for them, a future where one day perhaps they may not be silent. Who speaks for the voiceless? Nobody. But we must allow the silence of their voices to shape the future we choose. We must live and act and fight and love, so that they will have a place and one day a voice. And future generations, looking back, they will speak.

We should allow the silence of the voiceless to shape the future we choose.

As a youth work agency we are continually trying to find effective ways to include the perspective and voice of the young people we exist for in our work – both in terms of what we do and how we do it. In FYT we are trying to do this by ensuring that each of our staff spends a few days a year actively listening to young people – especially those who might be deemed at risk. We have been interested to find out how young people understand risk and what they say would make a fairer world for them.

Some young people have been concerned about police intimidation, being accused, being caught. Others have spoken about death being a risk for them; they also saw drugs and smoking as risks for themselves. Younger people mentioned paedophiles as a risk and feeling threatened walking around on their own. All ages spoke about the risk of all young people being tarred with the same brush and spoke of being dispersed when over a certain group size, even if they were only sitting talking to their friends. Personal safety was of concern, with one young person citing rape as a risk for them. Some young people mentioned that other young people's behaviour was a risk, especially when alcohol was involved.

There was a strong sense of young people feeling concerned about being moved on, being prevented from being seen in groups, yet not being able to change this, due to lack of facilities, and many cited the well-known phenomenon of "nowhere to go". Many just want to be with their friends; however, sitting on the streets exposes them to the risk of others' behaviour towards them, risks from adults, risks from police dispersal, and with a lack of power to change this situation. A significant number of young people cited the need for somewhere to go as a priority in terms of makinglife fairer.

A few questions for your own reflection

- I hope you find this feedback from young people of interest. However, I guess the big question is, how are you listening to young people yourself?

- If you are listening, what on earth are you doing about it?

Stories from the Edge 31:
Dave Swain

Simon was an angry young man I had met at the bus stop about eighteen months previously. We had been building trust with a group of young people when Simon turned up, f–ing and blinding one day, punching the windows and asking who we were. He was very uncertain of us, but with time, his barriers and aggression subsided. Just as I felt progress was being made, Simon, along with a few other guys, were sent down for eight months.

This hit everyone pretty hard. The group we were working with included sisters, girlfriends and best mates. We were able to support the group through this difficult time, but they kept us at arm's length – we were still relative strangers. We kept up with our weekly detached programme at the bus stops and the other areas of the town. Then the drop-in opened and many of the guys we were working with began using the place. After two months, Simon was released on "Tag" (wearing an electronic tagging device restricting his movements to a given location). It took a few weeks to get the trust built up again, but it wasn't long before he was in the drop-in twice a week. Informal chats developed into deep conversations.

After Christmas we were gutted to hear that Simon was facing another court case. The incident actually occurred prior to his doing time, and since then he had really sorted himself out. He was really getting a grip on his anger and had actually become the most calming influence on others who used the drop in.

For example, when there had been some damage and the fire extinguishers had been let off yet again, I asked everyone to sit round the table and discuss the problems. Simon was great. There was no need for me to lose my rag – Simon told everyone exactly what he thought!

But now he faced another stint in prison. He wasn't so gutted for himself; he was more worried about what it would do to his "Mam". Last time she had taken it badly and had been admitted to hospital.

Simon had done some bad things but underneath all the bravado, he had a heart of gold. He even preferred to do his time in Cardiff Prison (an old and massively overcrowded prison) rather than Parks, because it would be easier for his Mam to visit him. The whole court procedure was taking ages. The night before the start of the trial, Simon asked if we could all go bowling in Newport. So we piled into the cars on the Monday night and had a great evening bowling.

On the way back I suggested we finish off the night at the drop-in with a few drinks (soft ones!). We spent about an hour there, shooting pool and chatting. Earlier that day I had bought a bag of tea-lights. I asked everyone if they minded praying for Simon and the court case. I was nervous about how this would go down. They all knew I was a Christian and that the drop-in was part of my work for the Salvation Army, but this was the first time any tangible spiritual input had been put on the table.

The response was awesome. I explained that we would each light a candle of prayer and/or support for Simon, no matter what happened in court. Everyone lit a candle and a couple of us prayed some short, simple prayers. To be honest, that's all we could manage. I said they could take a candle home with them to remind them of tonight and even to pray with at home.

I noticed that Simon hadn't taken a candle. I was worried that I might have pushed things too far with him. I asked him why he hadn't taken one. To my amazement, he said he wanted to put it above the door in the drop-in and would pick it up when the case was over.

For various reasons, it took eleven months to get to sentencing. There had been lots of legal wrangling and plea-bargaining. In the end the more serious crime was dropped, if Simon pleaded guilty to two lesser ones, but he was still looking at between one and two years. Because of the changes in attitude and behaviour I had seen in Simon I had written a character reference for him, if nothing more than to maybe reduce the actual sentence.

The day before sentencing, Simon was over at my house helping me lay a patio in the garden. As we worked, Simon began to ask me how I got into youth work. He talked about an old run-down community centre up where he used to live. He had a vision of doing it up and re-opening it. There was something in it, but I explained that I had no extra hours to do something like that at the present. Simon asked how he could get into youth work – maybe he could do it.

We chatted through the various options and by the end of the day had come to the conclusion that it would be awesome if he worked alongside me in a trainee youth worker role. There was no money available but we could look into what New Deal could offer. We could get him on some training programme and he could do his practical with me. I promised that no matter what happened in court, I would look into how we could make this happen.

The day of sentencing arrived. I was all booted and suited; I had been advised that I would almost definitely take the stand. I sat in the public gallery along with his family. The prosecution outlined their case; it didn't sound good.

Simon was sat next to another boy who was involved. The judge was talking about fifteen months; you could feel the tension in the gallery. Simon looked round. I tried to give him a positive smile, but it was impossible – we were all gutted. Then the defence stood up. She brought the reference I had written to the judge's attention. He was seemingly impressed with the reference, and the fact that it came from the Salvation Army (it still has its uses!) seemed to hold some weight with him.

The judge read through it, then looked up at Simon. "We seem to have a paradox," the judge said. "The crimes as outlined by the prosecution describe a very angry, dangerous, nasty young man. However, I have in front of me a reference from the Salvation Army describing a responsible, mature, friendly and helpful young man." I couldn't help smiling to myself but was uncertain what would happen next. The judge continued, "I can only assume that I have a reformed character standing before me."

He carried on with his summing up. He started with a load of negative comments, but I had a gut instinct where it was going. I leaned over to my colleague, Jo, and whispered, "He's coming home!"

And sure enough, the judge swung over to positive comments before sentencing Simon to 120 hours of community service. The judge finished by saying, "It would not do the defendant, or society, any justice if this young man, who has turned his life around, was to be sent back to prison."

The gallery was in tears. I looked at his Mam, squeezed her hand and smiled. The relief on her face was fantastic to see. That night I joined them all in the pub to celebrate.

I am now at the stage where church, in its fullest sense, is being formed from scratch. God is active in the community and I love being a part of it.

Here is Simon's story in his own words:

> *God is active in the community and I love being a part of it.*

The hair on the back of my neck stood up as I looked at the judge. I felt a cold breeze in the courtroom that day. I was getting the blame, left, right and centre. But I'd made a deal with Jesus the night before. "I'll sort myself out, but please let me go home."

I heard the judge say something about fifteen months. I had a quick look over my shoulder and saw Dave, Jo, my family and my girlfriend, and wondered when I would see them next. Dave and Jo were Character References for me in court, and these had been the difference between doing time and going home, but it could have been a very different story.

I first met them in the Abertillery bus stops, about eighteen months ago, talking to those of us who hang around on the streets, and doing a questionnaire about a drop-in they were looking to open up. In those days I thought I was the man, but Jo and Dave were more genuine than a lot of people I had come across. I thought they were having a laugh when they talked about opening up a place for young people to hang out.

I was a ticking time-bomb around that time and was, sorry to say, really aggressive to them. Jo was obviously apprehensive towards us – she was a new girl in town. Dave was different – a lot more direct, not in an intimidating way, just not scared by the way we talked and behaved, that's his quality.

At first my girlfriend really hit it off with Jo and made no secret of it. I was always a bit wary, but that's why I decided to give Jo and Dave a chance. Sarah could never speak to just anyone. She did not know why she could speak to Jo and Dave, but I'm glad she did.

I continued to get along with Jo and Dave over the months, both on the streets and in the drop-in. Jo has been a tower of strength, taking me to court or just being a friend when I needed one. Dave – well, he's been brilliant. I helped him do his patio in his back yard. We chatted about how I could learn how to do youth work, get trained up and really get my life back on track. Come to think about it, where is my invitation to this barbecue he promised?

As far as the court case went, I received a 120-hours Community Punishment order, which I intend to do to the best of my ability and move on, putting my past behind me with the support of my family, girlfriend, and two strangers whom I now call friends. Thanks, Jo, and thanks, Dave, for my second chance.

A few questions for your own reflection

- How do you explore spirituality with people that aren't used to it?

- What measures would you put in place in working with "offenders" and what would you do if one wanted to work with you as a volunteer?

- This story has been intentionally interpreted and explored from the perspective of the "worker" and the young person that was involved – how do you get feed back from the young people that you work with?

Stories from the Edge 32:

Nigel Pimlott

There are few more frustrating things than unanswered prayer; except perhaps prayers being answered in a way that we are totally unprepared for and never expected!

Recently, I facilitated a training session for a church that had been praying for many years to have young people in their midst. After a big effort and commitment of resources, they had successfully engaged a group of local young people. The trouble was, they were not the young people they had thought about in their prayers.

These young people were lively, charismatic (but not in the theological sense!) and enjoyed chasing around the church building, causing chaos and damage, and (from all accounts) striking fear and trepidation into the minds of some of the older parishioners. As a result, the youth group was closed and the work was taken out into the community on more of a detached-youth-work basis in an attempt to preserve the sanctity of the building and the sanity of the congregation.

The young people, however, still wanted to come into the building, as they considered it a safe place and somewhere they could call "their own". As a consequence, they had started coming to the Sunday morning services. To some, this would be a great success – getting unchurched young people to come into church. After all, this was the initial goal of the project. However, this was not how the congregation viewed the proceedings. The young people had little regard for or knowledge of established protocols, were noisy at inappropriate moments, and appeared disrespectful of other worshippers. Some in the church were now positioned against the young people.

The training session revealed some factors that seem to sum up why the church often has problems working with young people and often fails them:

- They had sought to reach young people and had done so. They saw young people positively in terms of wanting to reach out to them via mission. However, they wanted the young people to come on their (i.e. the church's) terms and conform to their expectations and culture.

- They expected the young people to join in with their styles of worship.

- They expected that the young people would understand a traditional format of "church".

- They thought mission was easy and bore little cost!

- They expected that the young people would be able to differentiate between what was an "open session" and what was "Bible study".

- They thought the highest priority was to tell the young people about the gospel; they would then be converted and would behave as the church wanted them to. There was little understanding from some about building intentional relationships based on love, acceptance and trust. Doing so without preaching the gospel was seen as "not being of the Spirit".

- It was not clear what the church was trying to do with the young people once they had engaged them. There seemed to be no involvement of young people in governance, agenda setting, planning, etc.

- The church group wanted easy answers and didn't like me giving them the tools to explore possible ways forward. They wanted me to give them simple solutions to what were institutional and structural challenges.

I left the session feeling a mixture of sadness and frustration. So many churches would have longed for such an opportunity to work with such a group of young people. I had tried to be helpful and constructive, but I got the sense that some of the people at the training session had not liked what I had said.

So, if you are going to pray, make sure it is very specific, or else God could answer your prayers in a way that you did not expect and in a way that you are not prepared for. That's the business he is in – building the kingdom. His way, not ours.

A few questions for your own reflection

- Have you faced these kinds of issues, and if so, how do you respond as a youth worker?

- Is it desirable that youth workers act as "brokers" or "advocates" between young people and churches, and if so, how do you do it?

- What alternative strategies are there, and do they work?

Story from the Edge 33:
Diane Hall

This was the second time we had done a trip like this – an opportunity to take some young people away, develop our relationship with them, give their parents a break, give them a break from their environment, and enjoy the company of a welcoming Christian family. At least this time we were all nicely strapped into our car, rather than facing the prospect of a long train journey.

We were leaving about an hour later than planned, and we had to stop and get petrol. The petrol cap had refused to open with my key, but with my husband's it had been no problem. But of course, when we reached the petrol station a mile down the road, the cap refused to budge. I was just coming to terms with the panic and disappointment on the boys' faces when I thought I should pray about it silently, so I was praying away ("Lord, please open the petrol cap!"), and then I thought maybe I should get us all to pray. Now picture the scene – three boys who are completely unchurched, who giggle during any prayer, and who finish prayers with "Awoman" (get it?). They have never seen prayer as being even remotely relevant in their lives.

> They have never seen prayer as being even remotely relevant in their lives.

So I was in this dilemma. Do I suggest we pray out loud, and risk losing credibility if it doesn't open? Or should I just continue to pray silently? Eventually I just blurted out, "I think we should pray about this!" Apart from wide eyes and funny looks, there was no response. So I got us all to close our eyes and I offered up our plea to God. Of course, the cap then opened with ease.

Each boy had a different reaction. One said, "That's it – I'm becoming a Christian!" (We had a big chat with him about the costs and are awaiting further chats with him.)

Another said, "I'm going to pray for a million pounds now!" (I was able to explain why I believe God answers "petrol cap"-type prayers and wouldn't answer a "give me a million pounds now"-type prayer. So we had a great chat about God's character, our motivations for prayer etc.)

The other boy said, "You set that up!" (That made me laugh, but it made me sad too, as it showed how much scepticism there can be at such a young age.)

However, we have no doubt that this incident has made a *huge* impact on them, because it was the first thing they were telling people when we eventually reached our destination. It was a great opportunity for the young people to see how much God valued them, and how he really does answer prayer, and how he cares about us personally and intimately.

A few questions for your own reflection

- Is it realistic to be so blatant about asking for God's help in such everyday settings?

- Do you fear risking credibility if it seems like God has not answered the prayer?

- How would you have replied to each young person's response?

Notes

1. A. De Mello, *Prayer of the Frog*, vol. 2., IHS, 2002.
2. Thomas Merton, *The Wisdom of the Desert*, Darley Anderson, 1960, p. 59.
3. An expression used by Douglas Adams in *The HitchHiker's Guide to the Galaxy*, Pan, 1979. In an infinite universe, the Total Perspective Vortex provides a sense of proportion!
4. Marins, Trevisan and Chanona, *The Church from the Roots – Basic Ecclesial Communities*, CAFOD, 1983, p. 11.
5. Early church role play on *Mission and Young People at Risk* (training CD-ROM), Frontier Youth Trust, 2002. Available on 0121 687 3505 or www.fyt.org.uk
6. Philip Yancey, *What's So Amazing About Grace?*, Zondervan Publishing, 1997.
7. Vincent Donovan, *Christianity Rediscovered: An Epistle from the Masai*, 2nd edn, SCM Press, 1982.
8. Steve Beebee, *Youth Work Approaches to Gang Culture*, National Youth Agency, Dec. 2003, available from 0116 285 3700 or nya@nya.org.uk
9. Research carried out amongst Christians who are involved in working with gangs. A full copy of the research is available (free) at www.fyt.org.uk
10. Robert Beckford, *God and The Gangs*, Darton, Longman and Todd, 2004.
11. Peter Seaman, Katrina Turner, Malcolm Hill, Anne Stafford and Moira Walker, *Parenting and children's resilience in disadvantaged communities*, Joseph Rowntree research, 2007, http://www.jrf.org.uk
12. For example, see V. Browning, *Addressing public and media perceptions of young people – a compilation of initiatives within the UK*, on behalf of the YPN Foundation, November 2008.
13. D. Wells, *God in the Waste Land*, Eerdmans, 1996.
14. M. Riddell, *Threshold of the Future – Reforming the Church in the Post-Christian West*, SPCK, 1998.
15. R. Holman, *Kids at the Door Revisited*, Russell House Publishing, 2000.
16. For example, see Marins, Trevisan and Chanona, *The Church from the Roots – Basic Ecclesial Communities*, CAFOD, 1983.
17. See, for example, the works of Saul Alinsky, *Rules for Radicals, Vintage, 1971* or *Reveille for Radicals, Random House, 1969.*
18. See, for example, Phil Rankin's research, *Buried Spirituality*, Sarum, 2007; or Nigel and Jo Pimlott's *Youth Work After Christendom*, Paternoster, 2008.
19. R. Bakke, *Urban Christian*, MARC Europe, 1987.
20. See, for example, R. Holman, *Kids at the Door*, Blackett Press; *Kids at the Door Revisited*, Russell House Publishing, 2000; and *Resourceful Friends*, The Children's Society, 1983.